T0304014

ROUTLEDGE LIBRARY EDITIONS:
INFLATION

Volume 7

INFLATION AND SOCIETY

INFLATION AND SOCIETY

GRAHAM HUTTON

Routledge
Taylor & Francis Group

LONDON AND NEW YORK

First published in 1960 by George Allen & Unwin Ltd

This edition first published in 2016
by Routledge
2 Park Square, Milton Park, Abingdon, Oxon OX14 4RN

and by Routledge
711 Third Avenue, New York, NY 10017

Routledge is an imprint of the Taylor & Francis Group, an informa business

British Library Cataloguing in Publication Data
A catalogue record for this book is available from the British Library

ISBN: 978-1-138-65251-4 (Set)
ISBN: 978-1-315-62042-8 (Set) (ebk)
ISBN: 978-1-138-65709-0 (Volume 7) (hbk)
ISBN: 978-1-315-62150-0 (Volume 7) (ebk)

Publisher's Note
The publisher has gone to great lengths to ensure the quality of this reprint but points out that some imperfections in the original copies may be apparent.

Disclaimer
The publisher has made every effort to trace copyright holders and would welcome correspondence from those they have been unable to trace.

GRAHAM HUTTON

INFLATION
AND
SOCIETY

Ruskin House

GEORGE ALLEN & UNWIN LTD

MUSEUM STREET   LONDON

FIRST PUBLISHED IN 1960

PRINTED IN GREAT BRITAIN
in 11 point Juliana type by
SIMSON SHAND LTD
LONDON, HERTFORD AND HARLOW

FOR
LAVINIA
PHILIPPA
ALEXANDRA
'qui après nous vivez'

'There is no subtler, nor surer, means of overturning the existing basis of society than to debauch the currency. The process engages all the hidden forces of economic law on the side of destruction, and does it in a manner which not one man in a million is able to diagnose.'

The Economic Consequences of the Peace
by J. M. Keynes
London, Macmillan, 1919, page 220

FOREWORD

How inflation as a policy has come about in modern democracies, how it works, how to avoid it, and at what cost, is the theme of this book. It was written not for economists—who are mainly interested in the nature of the inflationary process itself—but for citizens knowing nothing of economics. So I have deliberately allowed my readers some repetition—mainly of examples or definitions—in different contexts here and there.

My main concern is the safeguarding of the democratic process as a guarantee for fuller realization of each individual's potentialities in a society. My chief concern here is therefore to make clear in non-technical terms what inflation does, both to society and to its individual elements, to weaken and hamper democracy. For that reason I began with the longest inflation in any one society of which we know anything: the Roman Empire.

Most of that study of ancient Roman society was delivered as a paper at the annual meeting of the Mont Pélerin Society at Princeton, NJ, in September 1958. For permission to reprint parts of my Introduction to Professor Wilhelm Röpke's *Welfare, Freedom and Inflation* (London, 1957) I am grateful to the Pall Mall Press and my friend Mr J. H. MacCallum Scott. I am also grateful to my fellow, familial economist Mr Robin Hutton, BA (Cantab.) for advice and help, and to my secretary, Miss Anne Burley, BA, for her patience and skill.

CONTENTS

PART I

WHENCE?

CHAPTER I

INFLATION PAST

It took all the centuries of humanity's painful advance up to 1914 to achieve democratic and representative self-government, universal adult suffrage and personal freedom. Within half a century of 1914, despite a phenomenal material progress which removed real poverty from among Western societies, that achievement was in retreat on a worldwide front, threatened by a monstrous regiment of State functionaries. The rule of law had collapsed, mined from within by the State's functionaries, breached from without by a citizenry overburdened with taxation and contemptuous of State agencies and authority. Democracy itself was in the discard. New and independent nations in other continents than that which had nourished democracy and liberty now turned their backs on both. In Europe, in the France of the Revolutionary tradition, representative government and democracy were cast aside. All the social institutions by which Western Europe and European North America could claim to have most advantaged mankind in its long struggle to escape poverty and the rule of the strong began to break down just as it reached prosperity and the rule of law to protect the weak. Just when man's supremacy over the blind forces of Nature seemed assured, when hard-won leisure and personal freedoms seemed to promise fuller and healthier human lives, men suddenly re-established a degree of State authority over all their activities unparalleled for a century and more.

The re-establishment of omnipotent, omnicompetent State authority in the modern world is more dangerous to personal freedom than any which has gone before. Man's supremacy over the blind forces of Nature stems from his technical achievements. All of these—powers unimaginable a lifetime or more ago—lend themselves aptly and easily to the exercise of centralized State authority through its farthest extremities in local bureaucracy. The individual man and woman—as producer and consumer, as citizen and unit of a family—is swamped beneath the new rules and regulations of centralized authority. Therewith come a narrowing of the bounds of personal development just when man's achievements should have widened them, a stereotyping of individual behaviour when new potentialities should have led to wider variations, and a banality which is already (wrongly) called vulgarity and materialism. Mankind now runs greater risk of seeing freedom whittled away by extension of the little-seeming, everyday, economic ways and means of the modern State than by any overt attack upon it. And of all instruments which subvert personal freedoms, inflation is the worst.

A continuous and rapid rise in prices is the clearest *manifestation* of progressive inflation. It has occurred in many countries in history, and in entire civilizations: among others, in ancient Greece, in the Roman Republic and in the classic case of the Roman Empire, in Renaissance Europe, and (in the era of World Wars) in the Napoleonic and the First and Second World Wars.

It is found with the growth of towns in later medieval Europe after the Black Death of 1348 and the consequent rise in wages and fall in available agrarian and urban labour supply. It is found again in the Iberian peninsula (and, later, throughout Europe) after the influx of gold and silver from the New World in the sixteenth century. In over-spending and near-bankrupt States like Germany after 1921 or 1945, or Hungary after 1944, it always shows up, production of money madly outrunning production of goods and services. In the entire trading world it occurs when the supply of international money suddenly expands, as at certain stages in the nineteenth century, when goldfields were opened up. And whenever local circumstances impel any government to inflate, debase, clip, devalue, or otherwise debauch the standard of value used as money (*e.g.* the regular debasements by Roman emperors, Anglo-Saxon monarchs before William the Conqueror, Plantagenet and Tudor kings, French Bourbons, and modern democratic and totalitarian governments alike) inflation becomes automatic and obvious. But the longest, progressive inflation of a single-standard currency is that of the Roman Empire.

The Roman Imperial inflation had clear-cut effects on Roman society. The effects endured longer than the society. Indeed, the Imperial inflation largely fashioned the local, feudal, agrarian communities on which later barbarian European nations were founded. The effects of the Roman inflation in breaking down cities and large-scale commerce were being endured in the Dark Ages of Merovingian, Carolingian and Capetian France; during the feudal epochs of Western Europe; and even in Norman and Angevin England, to say nothing of Lombard Italy. These effects of a much earlier inflation of a once reliable international currency were still felt during the painful period of the Early Renaissance, when Europe's modern towns and cities first re-emerged from a primarily self-sufficing agrarian feudal society, and grew up with new forms of trade and transport. Despite the evidence of some international trading adduced by such scholars as Dopsch and Pirenne, it is clear that feudal European society in the Dark Ages was locally hamstrung, tied to local lords and lands, where little money (if any) circulated. Surely the State Theory of Money was never so true as it was in the small societies, petty sovereignties, and little trading areas or markets of medieval Europe. 'The lord has the *ban*, but the King has the *arrière ban*.' The medieval King's power was as weak as his money and trade. That is the truth of feudal society.

The Dark Ages occurred because of what had happened between Augustus and Septimius Severus to a preceding *internationally*-organized society, largely dependent on international trade, in its turn based upon one main currency standard, and operated under one main system of international commercial law. One can plunge into Oertel, Brentano, Roztovtzeff, Vassiliev, Tenney Frank, Walbank, A. H. Jones, Colin Clark, and scores of other students' work on the economic breakdown of the Roman Empire; but in the end one comes away with three main conclusions about the causes and effects of the Imperial currency inflation from Augustus to Honorius.

The Centralized State

First, the Empire's State expenditure became intolerably and inefficiently burdensome, by way of increasing taxes. They had to be raised so high because most bulk trade, transport, defence, law, finance, and civil administration remorselessly became monolithic State enterprises. The exceptions for private trade were few, and progressively became fewer and more localized. The classic *parvenu*, the freedman Trimalchio in the *Satyricon* of Petronius Arbiter, was 'doing very nicely, thank you' out of Imperial monopolies. Urban and rural workers had to be 'frozen' in their jobs, which soon became hereditary—another adumbration of feudalism. Traders and merchants in the economic sphere, like the legions in the military, could only do well for themselves as State functionaries; and often their status became hereditary. Long before Pliny's statement. *'The big estates caused Italy to perish'* could become true, some cause had already created the big estates, the *latifundia*, as well as a bewilderingly rapid multiplication of rigidities, controls and controllers. That cause was the rapidly increasing taxation, levied mainly on the hitherto independent traders and farmers, the small men, to support the rapidly increasing expenditure of the rapidly expanding State machine.

It drove small yeomen and traders out of independent existence. It drove small farmers into dependency on others by their notorious 'flight' into slavery or clientism, or by the more genteel method of amalgamation with their neighbouring, bigger, larger-scale, and therefore more privileged, farming colleagues. It drove small artisans and traders into similar dependencies either as urban slaves or, more often, as members of big 'collectives' or 'colleges' of occupations, *i.e.* prototype guilds and trade unions.

Taxation was driven so high that it became almost sumptuary: *i.e.* it almost took away people's ability to own things. Nero, a psychopath, had said: 'Let's see to it that no one owns anything!'[1] But Caligula drove taxation to inordinate lengths: 'There was no class of commodities or of men on which he did not impose some tax or other. . . . On all eatables sold in any part of the city he levied a fixed and definite charge; on lawsuits and legal processes begun anywhere, a fortieth part of the sum involved, providing a penalty in case anyone was found guilty of compromising or abandoning a suit; on the daily wages of porters, an eighth; on the earnings of prostitutes, as much as each received for one embrace; and a clause was added to this chapter of the law, providing that those who had ever been prostitutes or acted

[1] Suetonius, *Lives of the Caesars*, Nero, XXXII: 'Hoc agamus, ne quis quicquam habeat'.

as panders should be liable to this public tax and that even matrimony should not be exempt."[1]

Gibbon's classic judgment of the Decline and Fall was that 'the stupendous fabric yielded to the pressure of its own weight'. But the process had begun early, when the fabric seemed still strong. As the demands of the proletariat-voters for 'bread and circuses' and those of the army for higher incomes drove taxes higher, a kind of 'Dutch auction' for votes set in. It ended by making the army the only elector of emperors, and the assassin of most of them. It also made it the destroyer of the cities and the citizens.

Depopulation of the countryside accompanied the urbanization of the early Empire. But as international trade languished with the progressive inflation, unemployment became rife inside the cities, which now shrank behind their new defensive walls. As money lost value, and as soldiers and bureaucrats multiplied and became the favoured classes of the State, the urban masses, mainly unemployed, had to be bought off with a Welfare State 'in kind' composed of free issues of bread, pork, and entertainments. The former governing class of the cities—the senatorial class—retired to larger and larger *latifundia* in the country, as the State's powers at the centre and in the cities grew.

The State—indeed, the Emperors—came increasingly to depend upon the goodwill of the legions and the votes of an idle rabble, both of them bought off by bigger depredations on the enfeebled tax-paying classes. As the unitary economic, defensive, administrative and legal territory of the Empire began to fall apart into feudal self-sufficing *civitates* surrounding the newly-walled cities, so an entire civilization fell apart. It dissolved, from the terrible third century onwards, into the dim outlines of modern European nations, and into our present ecclesiastical dioceses in Western Europe and the Middle East. The very word 'diocese' dates from this time. This process of dissolution took at least two centuries, and some say three.

It was accelerated, accompanied, and never once halted, by the progressive pushing of taxation—upon individuals—beyond what their 'value-judgments' were prepared to bear, through an ever-more-centralizing State. In the end, the State and the civilization dissolved into fragments, not because of barbarian invasions; indeed, the barbarians tried to maintain the civilization

[1] op. cit., Caligula, XL.

they admired; but because no one could be found to defend its integrity. That integrity had been inflated out of existence, out of defensibility.

The Politics of Favouritism

Secondly, behind this remorseless centralizing of all economic and administrative life, was an antecedent *political* cause. Politics is concerned ultimately with the exercise of power over human beings who are organized, by that power, in a society. Centraliza· tion of the State's power—in almost every walk of life—went on from the time of Augustus until the collapse in the fifth century. It could only be maintained, kept centralized, by a continual process of favouring, fiscally and financially, the power which had raised Emperors to, kept them on, and abruptly knocked them off the throne: that was, the army. Heavy taxes on a minority of taxpayers, *plus* debasement of the currency, gave the legions and the bureaucracy an advantage over all other classes, until they broke the Empire to pieces. Only one small privileged class—the senatorial—kept its former advantages *pari passu*, by contracting-out of its traditional task of government and going 'back to the land'. Thus it became the forerunner of the feudal barons.

Most taxpayers were urban. All of them were a tiny but economically important and productive minority. As their bur-dens grew, the *corps d'élite* of *decuriones* merely preferred slavery, flight, or the advent of the barbarians. This killed trade, com-merce, capital and cities. Outside the cities, in the countryside, legionaries in their camps and the biggest senatorial landlords on their *latifundia* were exempt from taxes. So progressive debase-ment of the currency and penal taxation to secure political power and support ended in the degradation and disintegration of the State. It was a vast paradox. Power itself, ultimately, deserted the State, the centre, and took to the smaller localities. Thus came the Dark and Middle Ages of servitude and status.

Government by Expediency

But there is a third factor, seldom mentioned by economic historians. It is the inherent paradox in this inflationary process: the *contradictory behaviour* of governments that persistently inflate. One can say—of Imperial Rome and many other inflating governments—that such governments undid as rapidly with their left hands whatever they were trying to do with their right. They always attacked—nay, are still attacking, after centuries— the surface symptoms rather than the disease. Such was Diocletian's notorious *Edictum de Pretiis* of 301 AD which made it a capital crime to raise prices anywhere in the Empire, and left us (you can consult it in the late Tenney Frank's transcription) a sobering standardization of all consumption and capital goods, their qualities, and their prices, throughout the then-known civilized world—from chariots and horses to ladies' underwear. Yet that decree was abandoned as bankrupt and inapplicable within two years. Not all of Diocletian's bureaucrats, soldiers and constabulary, under two Augusti and two Caesars, could have cut off the numbers of heads that would have had to roll. Economic laws and human nature defeated even Diocletian.

About the year 365 of our era the emperor Valentinian I faced even worse economic, fiscal and administrative problems than those of his great predecessor Diocletian. The burden of taxes on the decurions of the cities had become so crushing that entire *civitates*—that is, not only the walled city but the extensive agricultural supply-area around it—were rapidly and increasingly left without any *curiae* or local government. The reason, of course, was that the decurions of the *curiae* were legally and personally made responsible for finding the taxes. Naturally, as the huge tax-burdens for the top-heavy centralized State mounted, the individual decurions 'fled'. That is, they committed the first real *commendationes*, or voluntary personal servitudes, of the feudal ages. They fled to the rich landlords of the big rural estates. They became either their colons or their slaves. They even fled to the barbarians; and a strong Fifth Column—as we should now say—was formed from the educated city *élite* of the decurion class; for they intrigued to bring in the barbarians, in one Western city and its district after another.

The brief epilogue on 'The Economic Decay of the Roman World', based on Tenney Frank's last two lectures early in 1939 at Oxford and London, and closing the fifth volume of his *Economic Survey of Ancient Rome*, contains matter painfully familiar in contemporary experience:

'The ruler whose economic innovations proved ultimately most disastrous to the Empire was Septimius Severus . . . the important fact is that the rights of the citizens to independence and to property had been questioned, and habits of autocracy had been inculcated. . . . The havoc wrought was not due to a communistic revolution let loose against an ancient culture; it was due to the failure of efficient government at the centre of the State. . . . No recovery was possible except through the absolutism of Diocletian. . . . Typical of his régime is the imposition of a maximum limit both on the price of all wares for sale and on the amount of all wages, in order to keep wages as low as possible and to check the returns from industry. The declared purpose was to curb speculation when the State inflated the currency, but Diocletian attacked the inevitable result, not the cause, of inflation . . . the State which he saved lived under such conditions that it is questionable whether it was worth saving. At least, when the barbarians came on, the inhabitants of the Empire were in some doubt on this point, and many of them were glad to surrender, in the conviction that any new régime could hardly be worse than the one that they had endured.'

In despair, Valentinian I—by no means a fool, and certainly a brave emperor—decreed that the lictors should bring him three heads of decurions from each *curia* throughout one entire province, as an example. (Back to Diocletian's decree on prices, with a vengeance.) To this the prefect of the province, a certain Florentius, is said to have replied: 'Will your clemency be graciously pleased to command what we are supposed to do in the cases of those *curiae* in which there are no longer to be found even as many as *three* decurions?' The outcome was simple and, according to the chronicler, terse. The emperor's order was revoked—just like Diocletian's edict over sixty years earlier. But by this time the greatest Empire of European history was within fifty years of its collapse in utter ruin. After more than a millennium and a half the reverberations of that event have not died away.

CHAPTER 2

INFLATION PRESENT

Our era is surely one of supreme paradoxes. Never have so many human beings simultaneously sought peace, yet trembled on the brink of self-annihilation by war. Never have so many of them simultaneously sought national and individual freedoms and welfare on so wide and swift a scale, yet thereby set themselves on the brink of losing all freedoms and welfare, under the tyranny of the State and in the hands of a tiny oligarchy. Never have human beings as a whole been brought so close together and made so interdependent by their techniques, yet been sundered so violently by the hang-overs of antique dogmas, myths, slogans, sentiments and attitudes, both within and between nations. Never have so many human beings simultaneously reposed so great hopes on such costly education of their offspring, yet taken such irresponsible political action as must—ere their young people come to full maturity—end in removing from individual citizens the width of decision, and scope of self-determination, for which all education is intended. Never have so many of mankind hoped, vaunted and dared so much on the basis of technical advancement, yet simultaneously meekly acquiesced in the monopolization of the rapidly unfolding powers of science by new and privileged groups of State functionaries. And finally, never have so many human beings believed so fervently that old economic evils have been for ever eradicated, yet acquiesced so wholeheartedly in political and economic policies which must re-create those very evils on a wider scale. 'Paradox in Paradise', indeed.

In the sphere of economic policy in the latter half of our twentieth century, it is safe to say that the outstanding problem —the most widespread, least solved, most intractable, and least party-political economic problem—is that of inflation. It is a problem so wide-ranging in our world, so damaging to societies at all stages of social and economic development, that the surprising thing is not the number of articles, broadcasts and speeches on so sinister an influence, but rather the paucity of their effects in helping to solve it.

Inflation is a condition into which a country gets when its total of *money* income in any period rises faster than its *real* income of goods and services. For brevity's sake, we can accept as a working definition of inflation not the continuous rise in prices —for this is merely the effect—but the causal swelling of the stream of money at a rate faster than that of the stream of things (goods and services of every kind) on which this stream of money is spent. Something keeps that torrent of purchasing power (of all kinds) swelling at a faster rate than the slower-growing flow of goods and services turned out. Instead of the two streams keeping matched in force, and parallel in pace, so that prices stay reasonably stable in their general level (though not, of course, any given price of any given thing) the money-stream continues in spate, but the flow of goods and services goes in more sluggish wise, now swelling, now contracting, like a river suffering from alternating periods of drought and rainfall. As this instability between the two streams—this unbalance between the supply of money and the supply of things on which to spend it—has now gone on for nearly twenty years of war and so-called peace throughout the world as a whole, and shows scarcely a sign of being cured, it is worthwhile beginning at the beginning, and asking how and why the Great Changeover came about: the big switch from the years of deflation between the wars and up to about 1937, to the years of inflation ever since.

The State's Addiction to Inflation

Economists have a reputation for being obscure if not obscurantists, and for publicly disagreeing more than most specialists. But the significant thing about their attitudes to this world-wide inflation is that—whatever their nationality, party-politics, or non-economic aims—they agree, more widely and easily than on anything else, on the social, individual and international perils of too rapid an inflation. In short, there is among economists in the whole wide world a broad measure of agreement that if inflation goes ahead at too rapid a rate, the monetary system collapses, barter returns, the State must ration everybody (both consumers and producers), it must tax everybody (to get the savings for investment, which will not be made in money), and thus the country's international economic (and, therefore, military and diplomatic) powers are weakened, simultaneously with the enfeeblement of its productive efficiency at home. The point was well made by a British Chancellor of the Exchequer:

'I must draw the attention of the Committee and of the country to a real danger which, because we in this country have in the past successfully avoided it, is often ignored; the danger that, if incomes and prices rise swiftly and continuously, there may be a progressive loss of confidence in the value of money. Were such confidence to be lost we should be plunged into inflation of the most violent kind, which in other countries has on more than one occasion brought the whole fabric of their social and political life to the edge of disaster.'[1]

Even in Britain, where Socialist economists have publicly advocated inflation as an economic method of expropriating the 'capitalist classes', or the owners of property and the State debt, or 'private enterprise'—that is, as a means of bringing about a political and economic system run by the oligarchy of the State—those same economists also publicly admit that too rapid a rate of inflation would stultify their own political aims. So they have admitted the necessity of tempering the inflationary wind to the shorn lambs, at least for the duration of the lambs' wool-bearing lives.[2] And one or two of them have even confessed that too rapid a rate of inflation would also perpetrate a continuous fraud upon the retired and pensioners, upon the growing proportion of the nation which becomes pensioned year by year, and upon all savers and contributors to those State and private pension schemes upon which British Socialism now builds great hopes of electoral advantage in the future—whatever may happen to the millions of worker-contributors and their pensions in a future more remote. Thus, the differences about this world-wide inflation among economists—and about its degrees and effects in their various countries—turn upon much the same basis as a dispute between

[1] The Rt. Hon. Hugh Gaitskell in *Hansard*, House of Commons, Vol. 486, No. 83, Tuesday, 10 April, 1951, col. 840.
[2] See Chapter III, p. 48.

alcoholics or dope-addicts about what is 'a drop too much'.

From the Peace of Versailles, excoriated in Lord Keynes's *The Economic Consequences of the Peace,* until 1921 there was also such a world-wide inflation, the aftermath of a war. From 1921 to 1933-7 (varying from country to country) there was on the whole a world-wide deflation (with ups and downs in between). In that twenty years of war and peace and preparations for new war, Lord Keynes and most other economists came to view the outstanding economic problem of the world (Western and Eastern, developed or not) as that of *swelling the stream of money enough* to employ fully the unemployed men, machines and materials, lying around in the world-wide depression of prices. The words used then were 'over-saving', 'under-spending', 'public works', 'budget for a deficit', 'reflation': but they all amounted to the same thing—namely, inflation. Just as, today, economists do not use the 'bad word' deflation, but talk instead of 'disinflation', so, then, they did not use the 'bad word' inflation (for everyone remembered defeated Germany and its marks) but talked instead of 'reflation', *et cetera.*

Yet the Thing-in-Itself was the same. It meant swelling the stream of money by State action, by printing notes or otherwise increasing the official supplies of money and credit in the banking systems, so that people should have more of it, wherewith to buy lots more things, and so get the unemployed men, and under-employed machines, materials and farms, going again at full pelt. The clearest examples of this reflation in practice were in Hitler's Germany in 1933 onwards under Dr Schacht, in expansionist and imperialist Japan after the Manchurian adventure in 1931, and in Roosevelt's America of the New Deal which was re-floated by a reflation in 1933. The British reflation occurred after the de-valuation of the pound sterling in 1931 and the consequent housing boom and (later) the rearmament boom. 'The world that then was' rode headlong towards the second World War on a wave of reflation and rising prices.

From that time there has been no deflation, not even disinfla-tion, in the world; and all prices, on the whole and on balance, in all countries, have continued to rise. Since war ended, all our perils have been the opposite of deflationary. We have had over-investment on capital account by State authorities, over-employ-ment, over-spending by those same authorities on current account (a lot of it for Welfare State activities and bureaucracy), not enough savings. We got Keynesian methods and 'solutions' when we least needed them.

Inflations after 1945

The striking feature of the last twenty years of inflation is that most of it occurred *after*, not before, 1945. It has been, in short, an inflation of peacetime, or at any rate of war's aftermath, and not of wartime itself. There are many reasons for this. One is that the war took up whatever slack was still left in the ropes in 1939 : as war demands for war goods rose on all hands and supplies dwindled, men and machines and farms and materials were brought up to full capacity. When that full capacity itself was passed, forced savings had to be made in one warring country after another : most obviously, by rationing all round, by the State taking over most of the supplying of materials and even men, whether for armed forces or for what remained of civil life. So the flow of money soon began to swell, especially in the pockets of the people, for those who were not in the armed forces could not find goods to spend it on. Again, it was Lord Keynes who, in Britain, in his pamphlet *How to Pay for the War*,[1] openly suggested compulsory savings, taken from people's earnings, and called 'post-war credits', on the theory that they would be given back some day after the war, when the men and machines and materials and farms might become under-employed again. They never did. The State saw to that by over-investment, over-spending, and inflation.

Thus, even in the war the fears of post-war unemployment continued to haunt economists and statesmen. And when war ended, these fears were immediately and violently manifested, in Western Europe and even in America, although the war damage, the shortages, the running-down of countries' capital equipment and apparatus, the pent-up popular demands all over the world for decent standards of consumption and housing, and the general development of the technical improvements made in the war— all these reflation-demanding, these *inflationary*, influences were let loose upon the world even more quickly than the men and women (those who survived) could be let loose from the austerity of armed service.

[1] Macmillan, 1940, and see Chapter 6, p. 95.

Never, perhaps, in the whole course of economic history have so many economists been so wrong about so much, as they were between the end of 1944 and the end of 1947. They foresaw, they prepared for, deflation and unemployed resources consequent upon world-wide demobilization. Instead they got a breaking of all the wartime dams which had held up inflation. The streams flowing with money turned into torrents, while the streams flowing with goods and services (which the money was to buy) only gathered way slowly and in fits and starts. Thus began the wave of post-war inflation, everywhere: America, Africa, India, Russia, China, Europe. It continues to this day. Loss of purchasing power, currency crises and controls, wage-inflation, class and occupational and social tensions—all these wax with inflation, day by day, throughout the Western world and even beyond.

Consumption First

There were many other reasons, however, for the release of inflationary forces once the war had ended. The political revolutions of the world had been immense. They accelerated after the war. The Far East lived up to Field Marshal Smuts' prophecy a generation earlier, and went 'on the move' with a vengeance: China went Communist, India and many another ex-British dependent territory achieved independence and unleashed vast industrialization projects which were planned to be financed by inflation, new combinations of nations (on both sides of the Curtain) changed patterns of trade, and almost every nation (ex-belligerent or ex-neutral) set in hand ambitious programmes of capital development or of making good the ravages of war. Demands for foodstuffs and fodder, raw materials, sources of fuel and energy rose on all sides, and to levels unimaginable before or during the war. Whole peoples were tired and undernourished; whole industrial areas were badly in need of new equipment, communications, vehicles, buildings; homes did not as yet exist for families reunited; ports and ships were out of commission, run down, or lacking.

Then, again, as the reflationary (or inflationary) effect of the switch to full employment on civilian goods and services made itself felt, earnings rose and restraints upon spending were loosed. Everyone wanted consumer goods; yet the paramount need of the nations was rather for a continuation of saving so that the invest-

28

ment' (in capital, *i.e.* producers', goods) could be financed, wherewith the demobilized millions were to be fully employed in the arts of peace, or within which (houses) they were to dwell. Instead, and perhaps it was natural in the people if not in their rulers, almost everywhere—save in the defeated lands and in the Communist countries—the emphasis was first placed on production of consumers' goods and services; and in the capital programmes, in Britain in particular, the consumers' durable goods of houses took more than countries could really afford, in comparison with their basic needs of new *productive* capital equipment and communications.

But the most pressing inflationary force came from politics: it came from governments themselves, because of one aspect of the political revolutions in the world since 1939. That aspect was due to the enormously expanded powers of the State all over the world. As the State—a short way of saying the minority of politicians and officials—had expanded its powers to fight war or safeguard neutrality, it hung on to powers (as politicians nearly always do) after the war. In countries like Britain, Sweden, France and others, where Socialists had come to power in and after war, Socialism, with its century-old demand for 'State ownership of all the means of production, distribution and exchange', took unto itself even more powers over the lives, property, rights and freedoms of citizens, and over enterprises of all kinds, over trade, transport and commerce. Therewith, in such countries, the State took unto itself the duties of doing for citizens what they would otherwise have done for themselves. For these expenditures the State had to secure revenues.

Thus to the heavy post-war expenditures for the making good of wartime wear and tear, for demobilization, for new debts and new houses and new equipment of all kinds, were now added new spending on social services, for which new revenues (or 'contributions' *plus*, in many cases—especially the British—new taxes) were needed. In the bulk of these nations—made up of the beneficiaries of the new social services, on balance, who contributed less than their share—consumers' everyday spending was thus subsidized; while for the minority in these nations, which paid most of the direct taxes and contributions and used to do most of the personal saving before the war, spending power and saving power alike were reduced. Thus, all the expanded powers of States over citizens in the Western nations had an inflationary effect on balance, added to the other inflationary effects. And as these nations prided themselves on still being democracies—defined as government by mere majority of votes—whatever political party or coalition got power found itself faced with the dilemma of halting inflation by measures likely to lose it power, or of keeping the power at the cost of continuous inflation. The choice was only too fatally easy.

Inflation in Germany

The German people in two successive generations learned about the inherent perils of inflation the hard way: after successive defeats in wars. The inflation after the first war robbed them, in addition to the war dead, of a responsible *élite* or *bourgeoisie* or class of leaders, independent-minded because of independent private property yet loyal to State and society because they guaranteed to them both property and responsible leadership. Instead the Germany of Social-Democracy between 1919 and 1933 led to one Leader, and after him the deluge. That was one lesson of one inflation. If, today, the younger generation of Germans, guaranteed its freedoms and property and abilities and rights to earn, refuses to enthuse either about re-creating a German army, or about policies leading to and based on inflation, outsiders should at least understand it.

It is only a dozen years since Dr Erhard and his able economic advisers ended the second German inflation after the second war, and established that Deutsche mark which is at present the strongest and freest West European currency next to the Swiss franc. And outsiders should also observe that German Socialism today flees and abjures policies necessarily leading to inflation, even at the cost of disalignment from its British Socialist comrades. It is evidently not prepared to trade what Dr Erhard miraculously built up in less than a decade, on the basis of a prostrate and defeated people in a bankrupt economy, for a mess of inflationary pottage, further inflated by politicians' promises that can never be fulfilled. Germans know a lot, which will last them for a long time, about inflationary disillusion.

Inflation in France

The French people have been plagued with inflation and many

successive devaluations of the franc for forty-five years. Their economic recuperability as a nation never failed to astonish outsiders after 1815 and 1871—and is as astonishing as ever. It is founded on a rare, remarkable balance for any modern society: that between industry and agriculture. That balance is much more equal than the relationship between industry and agriculture in the United States (where industry o'ertops agriculture and heavily subsidizes it), Australia (where agriculture still o'ertops industry and subsidizes industrialization), Germany (which closely resembles the USA), Italy and Japan (like Germany), and Britain (which is the most heavily industrialized of all).

The basic economic strength of France renders her less vulnerable to the swings of world prices and trade. She is not so dependent on them. This enables her to sustain for surprisingly long periods such running sores as inflation itself, the enduring trouble in her North African territories, and the thirty-year succession of impotent democratic governments which ended with the fall of the Fourth Republic in 1958 and its supersession by the almost monarchical powers of the De Gaulle *régime*. Only with the advent of that kind of *régime* were the 'sound money men', particularly MM. Pinay, Rueff and Baumgartner, empowered to stabilize the purchasing power of a new, much-depreciated franc and thus make it reliable, and calculable for savers and investors. Only then did the franc become valuable to foreigners as well as to the French, the economy surge forward at a rate of growth unparalleled in fifty years, and private capital come out of hoards at home and abroad and be put to productive uses. The moral of the forty-five-year-long French inflation, and of the *débâcle* of democracy which (more than any other single factor) it finally caused, stands clearly writ in recent memories. In its way it is as striking as that of the thirty-year-long German inflation between 1918 and 1948.

American Inflation

Against the French and German inflations that of the United States has been insignificant. Dollar prices have not risen like all other prices, and dollar incomes have risen with American output per head. But inflation has not been negligible to Americans, despite American economic growth. It has only recently—since 1959—become the biggest single economic fear they profess.

They have as yet no confidence in their ability to keep up the fabulous rate of American economic growth and of full employment without inflation.

So far the US dollar, devalued and based on gold at $US 35.00 to the ounce as long ago as 1933, has not been devalued again. Its depreciation due to inflation (since war began in 1939), the fall in its purchasing power, has been no greater than that of the Swiss franc, and far less than that of the Swedish krona. (The currency of this other leading neutral industrial democracy has accompanied the pound sterling in its alarming inflationary losses and devaluations.) Partly, like France, the USA gains some stability for its prices by producing all its own food and most of its own raw materials, fuels and other primary products. It is a highly industrialized democracy—though not *proportionately* as industrialized as Britain—and by far the most efficient manufacturing country in the world. Its average output per head, and therefore average consumption per head (material standard of living), for hours of work is double that of the next countries on the list (Canada, Australia), more than double those of Britain, more than four times those of Russia, more than eight times those of India, and more than ten times those of China. And it is a two-party democracy *minus* any Socialism, Communism, other collectivism, or *dirigisme*.

As a politico-economic system it ranks with Switzerland alone in constitutionally guaranteeing its citizens' personal, corporate and economic freedoms in property and trade and exchange and safeguarding them by the powers not of elected Governments but of Law Courts. These two written democratic Constitutions are, happily for their citizens, extremely hard to change. They cannot even be changed by a simple majority vote. For these reasons it is worth noting the significant preservation of basic economic freedoms in the USA and Switzerland (both Federal Powers) alongside the least State centralization and inflation of their currencies to be seen in all modern industrialized democracies. Yet not even in America or Switzerland have their governments—more successful so far in holding inflation at bay than any other democratic governments—been able to banish the fear of future inflation.

Inflation in Less Industrial Lands
Of inflation in Latin American lands it is not necessary to write

much. They are the laboratory of classic inflations. Their currencies have lost and still lose their purchasing power more swiftly, change their names more frequently, and cause more social and political upheavals than any others on earth. Their politics and societies are accordingly in continuous flux. No group, class, property or profession 'stays put'. Nothing is reliable or dependable. *Ce n'est que le provisoire qui dure.* Life is lived there, and business done, on the basis of provisional permanence or permanent provisionality. It clearly has not made for rapid economic growth, though for certain temperaments it is enjoyably stimulating.

Among the non-industrialized countries in the free half of the world—many of them having only recently gained their full and sovereign independence—an ambitious, if understandable, nationalism has often combined with an equally understandable straining after breakneck industrialization. This latter cannot even today—and never could—be achieved at breakneck pace: witness the forty-two-year-long travail of the Russian people. Accordingly in such still 'underdeveloped countries' the possibilities of private saving and investment have seemed to their governors too small and too slow. Open inflation as an instrument of policy has been chosen, avowedly a method of 'forcing savings'. Of such countries India, with her three Five-year Plans all reposing on a large amount of deliberate inflation, is the biggest example.

CHAPTER 3

THE GREAT BRITISH INFLATION

After a war in which she fought as long as any combatant, and longer than most, Britain might have expected to be poor, weak and negligible. Her people might have expected to live on lower standards than before the war; to lose exports and therefore imports; to be unable to afford adequate defences, an ambitious and costly Welfare State, and vast new investments in housing, fuel and power, and the modernization of industries. Instead, within a decade and a half, Britain—with aid from the United States and Canada—restored sterling to its place as the currency in which over one-third of the world's trade is financed, doubled the *volume* of her exports, and raised the consumption of three quarters of her people by some 30 per cent compared with what it was in 1938.

Yet during those fifteen years most people in Britain—whatever their ages, jobs, incomes or politics—sensed that something was wrong at the economic heart of the country. Most of them, in Prime Minister Macmillan's words, had 'never had it so good'. Certainly that was true of the three quarters of them who lived by wages and lower salaries. They were now consuming roughly one-third more food, leisure, pleasures, travel, gadgets and other items in their rising standard of life than they did on average in 1938. They might well have thought: 'If this is what inflation, full employment and repeated sterling crises do for us, long may they flourish!'

But most of them did not feel that way about it. They naturally pressed for all they could get as workpeople to protect themselves from a lowering uncertainty—while criticizing anyone else (their employers, for instance) who did the same. They knew that around them, in or out of their own workplaces, great economic wastes and inefficiencies were occurring every day. They saw poor—even bad—performances of both men and machines. They took part in restrictive practices of many kinds, produced shoddy work, and permitted careless treatment of costly capital apparatus. They saw wrong managerial decisions being carried out. They soon began to feel anxious, annoyed, confused. Some of this dissatisfaction found expression in the 1959 General Election, which came after the first full year's stability in the cost of living since the end of the war nearly fifteen years earlier.

This underlying malaise was not caused by any of the traditional economic anxieties of life. For example, very few had grounds to fear unemployment. Although the working population had risen since 1938 by more than one-fifth the country nevertheless had full employment (by any definition) throughout the fifteen years following the war. There were three periods of slight increase in the numbers of workers out of a job: the economic crises of 1947, of 1951-52, and the autumn and winter of 1958-59. Even then the total of unemployed never rose to the long-run *average* 'revolving' unemployment figure of 3 per cent which Lord Beveridge and his advisers had taken as normal in their recommendations when war ended.[1] While there were of course greater regional variations, average unemployment stayed around 1·5 per cent of the working population after the first postwar sterling crisis. For most of the time there were more vacant jobs notified to Employment Exchanges—to take no account of those not notified—than unemployed men or women to fill them.

Static incomes cannot have been a major cause of anxiety for most of the working population. From 1938 to 1958 the total of wages in the country had multiplied by four and a half times. There was a relatively greater increase in the number of salary earners than wage earners, and the total of salaries paid also rose to four times its 1938 level. But incomes from rents, dividends (distributed profits) and interest only doubled in money terms since 1938. They did not keep pace with prices.

Levels of consumption of real things—goods and services— were much higher than before the war for three quarters of the British people. Since 1938 the amount of money in the hands of the public had risen over threefold. Between the end of the war and 1958 it nearly doubled and even after 1951 it rose by about one-third.

[1] See Chapter 6, p. 95.

Prices—the 'cost of living' measured by every known method —rose from an index of 100 in 1939 to at least 270 in the middle of 1959. (Some measurements show the figure nearer 300.) This meant that any income, to maintain its pre-war purchasing power, should have been multiplied by between 2·7 and 3·0. Most wages and salaries did more than that. Rent, dividends and interest, on the other hand, did not. Nor could the higher *earned* incomes keep pace with the inflation, because much heavier taxes on income cut down the higher earnings ('progressive taxation'). So the mass of the nation—excepting those earning higher incomes or living on income from property—was living on a much higher standard of real consumption than that of 1938 or earlier. Indeed it was the highest standard ever achieved for the British people.

Internal against External Demands

The cause of anxiety was less obvious, more insidious, than any discontents of this nature. Between the end of the war and the end of 1959 the pound lost over two-fifths—nearly half—of its domestic worth. In only two years out of the period between 1945 and 1960 did the internal value of the currency remain anywhere near stable: between September 1955 and September 1956, and again during 1958-59. It was this unparalleled, quick and continuous fall in the purchasing power of the pound that brought home to most people, particularly housewives, that all was not well, despite the improvements in standards of living.

The purchasing power of a currency is governed primarily by the interaction of the flow of money in the public's hands and the flow of available goods and services on which this money can be spent. But in the twenty years between 1939 and 1959—while the working population grew by only one-fifth, but the amount of money in circulation more than four times—the real quantity of goods and services *available for all purposes within the country* also increased only by about one-fifth. True, total national output rose by two-fifths or 40 per cent between 1939 and 1959. But after the war Britain had to pay—that is, to export—to the outside world one of those two-fifths of her extra output, without being able to buy any more imports with it, in order to meet the new post-war debts and other financial burdens incurred during and after the war. These post-war burdens were the real economic sacrifices imposed on Britain because of the war. They laid a heavy responsibility on those charged with the management of the economy.

In the post-war world Britain faced a number of urgent, often conflicting obligations. First, she had to meet debts incurred during the war to friends and allies mainly in the Commonwealth and sterling area (the older Dominions or new ones like India) and to other countries (*e.g.* Egypt).

Secondly, she had to honour and be ready to repay debts incurred after the war. These included the Canadian and US loans of 1945-46; later loans from the US; 'sterling balances' earned by exports of cocoa, tin, rubber, etc, from her remaining Colonies; deficits incurred in trading with other European countries; and borrowings from the Export-Import Bank in the US and the International Monetary Fund to reinforce the dollar reserves whenever these came under regular and extra strain.

Thirdly, beside these contractual obligations she had to meet *relatively* higher post-war prices of all her vital imports of raw materials. This was because the terms of trade had turned against Britain since 1939. It meant that relatively more manufactured goods had to be exported to buy the same volume of raw materials. And more raw materials were needed anyway to sustain a larger population, higher employment, increased debts, and a regularly boosted rise in the consumption of three-quarters of the nation. After 1957 the terms of trade began to move a little more favourably for Great Britain and to this extent the problem was eased; but the inflationary demands for more resources than were available kept on increasing.

Fourthly, Britain had to meet practically the full cost of all her imports by paying as she went along, instead of getting one-fifth of them *gratis*—as before the war—in payment of interest and dividends on the investments abroad of her former citizens in the nineteenth century. The most 'paying' of those investments had been sold to fight the war. What were left did not yield enough to pay for one-twenty-fifth of the country's necessary imports at post-war prices.

Fifthly, she had to meet the increased needs of the less-developed countries in the Commonwealth and sterling area for capital and for capital apparatus and equipment made in Britain. In helping to develop the resources of food and materials in those countries Britain and the sterling area were rendered less dependent on dollar or other 'hard currency' countries for their supplies.

Sixth and lastly in addition to all this, Britain had to meet the doubled post-war burden of expenditure abroad for her own defences and those of her associates in the Commonwealth and her allies in the common defence of the free half of the world (*e.g.* NATO).

To put all this another way: Britain had full employment, a working population one-fifth bigger than in 1938, a vast and rising outflow of money wages and salaries and paper-profits of companies, and heavy new investments in the productive equipment of her industries. She also managed to double the volume (not just the value) of her exports. But those exports could only buy a slightly bigger volume of imports than were taken before the war for a smaller nation, less fully employed, and on lower standards of life.

There were thus three ugly faces presented by Britain's enduring post-war problem. First, one half of the increase in total output over its 1938-39 level had to go out as exports, but could buy no imports at all. Therefore roughly 20 per cent of the extra 40 per cent of Britain's output *was not available inside the country to increase the capital equipment or consumption of anyone,* whether public body or private person. Secondly, the remaining half of the increase in total output over 1938-39 had to cover all the urgent post-war (and continuing) needs of both social and productive capital—houses, schools, hospitals, roads, railways, coal-mines, steel, electricity, ships, ports, atomic energy, and all the replacement and expansion of factories and their productive apparatus belonging to the private enterprise of 'manufacturing' (which makes all Britain's exports). And thirdly, despite all this, official and private figures show that three quarters of the bigger population were consuming more than those three quarters did in 1938-39—from an *average* of 10 per cent more in as early a post-war year as 1950 to an *average* of 30 per cent more by 1960.

It does not take an economist or mathematician to spot the joker in this pack. Post-war Britain faced burdensome post-war debts, the penalties of war. Taxes were pushed to penal heights on all the more productive persons and concerns. Yet for most of the fifteen years following the war the mass of the nation consumed far more and scarcely saved; and by everything from rapid inflation to an ambitious system of State welfare for the masses (raised by penal taxes) mass-consumption was encouraged. The small minority who formerly had saved, no longer saved as much, and (due to taxation and the continuous inflation) even consumed capital. The whole nation had big new burdens to shoulder. It repeatedly ran away from shouldering them—so every two years it plunged itself into an economic crisis. In desperate struggles to shift these burdens from the bulk of the nation on to the few, from the organized voters to the unorganized, Britain had persistent inflation. Governments and people apparently preferred it that way—at least until 1958.

Consumption against Investment

Britain faced the post-war years with a large number of urgent and competing demands on that never-adequate part of her resources which was available for all purposes inside Britain. She had to build houses, schools, hospitals, and other good things for her population to use over a long period of time—these can be called 'Welfare State capital', or 'social capital', or sometimes 'consumers' durable goods'. Enormous sums were spent on these necessary and desirable things. About one-fifth of all savings made by the nation between the end of the war and 1958 went into housing. All the *productive* capital needed after the war by nationalized industries and private enterprises to modernize and expand productive apparatus for the larger working population —to provide buildings, highways, railways and power stations of all kinds as well as the most modern machinery and equipment— made further heavy and urgent demands on the nation's available resources. Indeed, these two groups of demands alone would not have been satisfied even if the whole of Britain's available extra 20 per cent of output compared with before the war had been devoted to such necessary capital purposes. As it was, between 1948 and 1958 three-quarters of the bigger working population and all their dependents consumed—not saved but *consumed*—on average about one-quarter more goods and services per head than before the war. This increased consumption by itself would have run away with most of the extra output available. It would have left ludicrously little to cover the urgent capital needs.

The result was that—even if one includes houses, schools,

39

etc, as 'capital'—Britain did not save and invest as much of her national output in the post-war years as the USA, Germany, and other industrial countries. True she began to pick up in this respect after the Budget of 1954; but she then ran headlong into the fourth post-war crisis of inflation and overstrained resources, mainly due to the superimposition of the '300,000 new houses a year' programme upon the industrial re-equipment programme. Not until 1958 did the position become more favourable. Over the bulk of the post-war decade and a half Britain, although in a less favourable position in the world than in 1938, was able easily to maintain full employment and pay-packets (her people had to work more for foreigners). In addition, the Welfare State gave big mass subsidies not to saving but to consumption. Far more savings than were available were needed for urgent new capital programmes; yet penal taxes took a lot of the savings of businesses and private individuals in order to cover *current* State expenditure (not on capital assets) at a time when inflation, anyway, was working against saving.

It is therefore something of a miracle that so much was achieved. Exports were doubled, imports restrained; consumption for most of the people raised, leisure and enjoyments increased; and the burdens of national and international defence were borne. In addition, sufficient was saved to invest in vast new housing projects on public money, in enormous capital programmes for coal-mining, railways, electricity and other nationalized industries (also on public money), and especially in the later 1950s in a wide and overdue modernization of the productive capital equipment in most of private enterprise. How, then, did Britain and her people manage to do so well? Was it all really a recommendation for inflation as a policy?

Who and What Went to the Wall?

The solution to the apparent puzzle lies in four main facts. First, the nation's needs of all new productive capital—to equip it to meet *all* demands on its productive capacity—simply were not met. Although about 2,800,000 new post-war houses were built up to 1958 (mainly on taxpayers' money, and let at subsidized rents which also therefore artificially boosted consumption) not enough new hospitals, schools, colleges, etc, were constructed with public funds. While many new electricity stations and atomic energy plants were allocated public money, for the first two-thirds of the post-war decade and a half at any rate not enough steel was produced from an industry which was first politically interrupted, disorganized and handicapped, and only forged ahead on its own funds and on borrowings from the market towards the end of that period. Although almost £540 million of public money was sunk in coal-mining between 1951 and 1958 total coal output over the eight years never reached the level of 1938.

Not until the end of the fifteen years following the war did the State make even a bit of progress in improving the capital of the railways and highways and in expanding their capacity. Indeed the state of the national highways and of the railways' tracks, rolling stock, traction stock and performance was a matter of common public derision. As compared with the highways and railways of other industrial nations, big or small (USA, Holland, Germany, Belgium), Britain entered the 1960s with woefully few stretches of first-class highway and with a woeful railway service. In short, so inadequate were the savings made by the entire nation over the major part of the period that they came nowhere near providing all of the resources needed for urgent modernization. If Peter had his capital needs met, Paul had to go without; and the lack of Paul's output was a source of trouble.

Secondly, the State—under successive Governments—took the responsibility of deciding between the covering of Peter's or Paul's capital needs. Until the end of 1954, ten years after the war, private industries' needs of new capital went to the end of the queue. Yet 100 per cent of Britain's exports came from private enterprise, overwhelmingly in manufacturing. When added to the State's demands for capital, the amount of new capital which private manufacturing industry could get—out of the half (or less) of its profits left to it by the Inland Revenue, or out of people's savings (insurance funds, etc) put into the capital market—outran the total of the nation's savings. In fact, successive Governments only managed to cut the nation's over-all investment to the cloth of savings in three years out of the first fifteen after the end of the war, in spite of the heaviest taxes in the free world, frequent budget surpluses 'above the line', and continual controls over capital issues. In nearly all post-war years there were not enough funds for all the State's needs on capital account, to say nothing of the capital needed by all of British private enterprises.

The method adopted by governments to cope with this situation itself contributed to the continuation of the nation's problems. Instead of borrowing at high interest rates at long or medium term from savers; instead of cutting down their own demands for cash for current and capital purposes (including of course defence); instead of raising taxes even higher (which admittedly would have defeated itself by stopping saving and encouraging the spending of savings) they had the money printed. By 'borrowing short'—that is by issuing IOUs (Treasury Bills) or 'floating debt' (renewable *every three months*)—the first Labour Governments after the war greatly expanded the liquid assets of the banking system, which consist largely of these Government short term bills. The more the banks or the money market advanced cash to the Government the more bank credit could be expanded and granted to others on this growing basis.

This deliberate 'cheap money' policy of the Labour Governments forced down all interest rates, owing to the superfluity of money and credit and to the comparative rarity of goods and services. Government borrowing by gilt-edged bonds was done at a $2\frac{1}{2}$ per cent long-term rate—a low price which (after the Chancellor of the Day, Dr Hugh Dalton) earned them the sobriquet of 'Daltons'. The reckoning bided. Within a decade they stood below one-half of their issue price, when the long-term rate of interest had risen to over 5 per cent; and all lenders to the Government in the later 1940s lost half—and more—of their capital by the end of the 1950s.[1]

Nevertheless the succeeding Conservative Governments dared not cut or 'fund' this vast 'floating debt', to change it into medium or long term debt. Throughout the post-war decade and a half it remained at five times its pre-war total. That goes a long way to explain the fourfold increase in the cash and credit held by the nation. If this short-term, floating debt had been 'funded' into medium or long-term debt, which does not form the basis for bank credit, interest rates would have greatly risen and both State and private activities would have had to be curtailed. But the economy would have been on a sounder basis of values, and deci-

[1] See Chapter 4, p. 59.

sions could have been better taken on which lines of investment to pursue.[1]

As a result of this governmental policy enabling the supply of cash and credit to expand (in order to meet the State's bills) the stream of money flowing into pockets and bank accounts continually swelled. The better-run concerns could cover all demands for higher wages. Profits rose. The inflationary booster went on maintaining full employment, shortages, profitability (even for inefficient firms) from rising prices, a rising cost of living, new wage demands, etc. As the inflation in the supply of money kept up full employment and there were not enough resources to meet the rising money demands at home, 'money chased goods'. Prices steadily rose. Then wage demands were again pressed, and conceded out of inflationary profits. And so it went on. As prices rose more money was required in the system. Partly this requirement was met by the banks and printing press; partly by pushing money and credit around faster, making it do more work in a week or year. As in all inflations therefore the velocity of circulation of money rose as the inflation progressed.

Costs of Inflation

The various governments occasionally tried to reduce inflation by holding down the capital demands of all private enterprises that were not judged to be 'dollar earners' or of highest priority. Of necessity this was an almost impossible task for the State to undertake in a democracy. But in Britain it was doubly damaging because it involved deciding who should supply whom, with what, in a private-enterprise sector producing over three quarters of the country's output *and all her exports*. Such decisions inevitably led to arbitrary injustices and—worse—to inefficiencies. Not even the State industries and agencies got all the new capital they needed.

Next the State, in order to finance all its own continued expenditures, had to keep all taxes on productive industry, incomes, pleasures and necessities of life for the mass of the people crushingly high. This in its turn led to inflationary demands for higher wages and other incomes, and even for subsidies for con-

[1] See pp. 73 and 78-87 and the remarks of Professor F. W. Paish, Mr L. W. Robson and the author in their joint evidence before the Radcliffe Commission, Minutes of Evidence, Vol. 3, p. 189.

sumers. People got used to 'discounting taxes and inflation'—
i.e. reckoning the real, net, levels of income, reward, or price, and
demanding more to cover all taxes. One-half, on average, of any
profits made by any person or private or public company was
taken in taxes.

The State also had to raise continuously the employers' and
employees' contributions to National Insurance in order to pay
for the rising costs of the Welfare State, including the necessary
increases in pensions to offset the inflation. These too were taxes.
On average over the 1950s contributions to the Health Service
alone fell short by £500 million a year of covering the expenditure
on goods and services in running that portion of the Welfare
State. This deficiency was roughly equivalent to an extra half-
crown on the average standard rate of income tax, and had to be
found by all taxpayers.

Finally both Labour and Conservative Governments had continuously to raise the taxes on leisure pastimes or pleasures of
the majority of the people and spasmodically to place restrictions
on hire-purchase. Petrol, tobacco, motor cars, motorcycles, domestic apparatus, radios and television sets and a host of other products used in the enjoyment of leisure suffered taxation, or controls, or both, at levels unparalleled in the free half of the world.

Certainly this State-fostered inflation was keeping up employment, but keeping it up as an overstoked furnace keeps up pressure in a boiler. The safety of the place and the people around
depends on the tolerances inside the boiler and the degree to
which it is overstoked. The indications of overstoking in Britain
were the biennial crises for sterling (four in eleven years), rising
prices, social tensions, and the continuous deterioration of the
UK's place, relative to other countries, in world markets for
manufactures. They were the evidence of resources overstrained
for far too long, of a people overburdened by its own apparatus
of State.

Debtors' Devices

The third clue to the puzzle of Britain's achievements, in spite
of her difficulties, lay in maintaining a high volume of trade
inside the sterling area. Half her doubled exports went to other
sterling area countries. Much of this trade, however, was in repayment of wartime and post-war sterling debts which she owed.

Yet by 1960 the total of the UK's sterling debts had not been significantly reduced. The inflation had merely slashed the debt-holders', the creditors', purchasing power. Since a high proportion of the cost of any export made to repay sterling debt has already been circulated (by the time the export is made) as wages and other incomes inside Britain, it is still circulating as purchasing-power at home. Almost all of it goes in consumption and is not saved. Far more money was thus pushed into the system than goods for it to buy, for at least half the extra goods had been sent abroad in repayment of debt.

However, a gradual improvement in the terms of trade set in after 1955; and the opening at the end of the 1950s of a new stage in international trade in general was another help to Britain. Although one effect of her exports to the rest of the sterling area was inflationary (in so far as it was in settlement of debt) she benefited from the high volume of international trade which she and the rest of the world were able to maintain.

The cause of rising costs and prices inside the United Kingdom, and of the falling value of the pound, was the continuous over-spending, both on current and capital account, by governments and State undertakings—over and above, first, their revenues and, secondly, their long-term borrowings of current savings through the capital markets. Governments 'kept the heat on' in the national boiler by expanding the basis for the creation of money and credit. More money flowed than goods and services—available for all purposes in the UK—to offset it. Had the flow of goods and services *available for all domestic uses* matched the continuously rising outflow of money, the evils of the inflation would have been avoided; or, if it had nevertheless occurred, it would not have been Britain's fault.

What happened in other sterling area countries (*e.g.* India) had its effects on the process as well as what was done—or was not done—in Britain. When other sterling countries imported more than their exports and borrowings could pay for, they also weakened sterling. Between 1950 and 1958 the rest of the sterling area taken together failed to balance its current trade with the non-sterling world by a total of roughly £1,000 million. Much of this deficit was covered by investments in the sterling area from America, Britain, and other countries, and by outright charity (*e.g.* to India). Over this period, therefore, Britain was helped by her partners in the sterling pool, to the extent that she ran up, and kept up, short-term debts to them ('sterling balances') which she then lent to others at long-term. It was an odd and dubious procedure, and scarcely one that could be relied on to endure as more of her former dependencies (to whom she owed debts) became independent.

Had every other nation, within and without the sterling area, inflated as fast as Britain, it might not have mattered: what was lost on the international swings might have been gained on the international roundabouts. Had Britain managed—as Germany did—to increase her productive efficiency (productivity of machines and men) as fast as, or faster than, the outflow of money, the relationship between goods and services on the one hand and of money on the other could have been balanced. Prices would then have been more stable. They might even have fallen while those of the products of other nations continued to rise. Then, like Germany, Britain would have been increasingly able to expand her imports to raise her people's welfare; to discharge her foreign debts with more exports; to make investments overseas to develop the Commonwealth and other underdeveloped resources; and to accumulate gold and dollar reserves against the rainy day. As it was, from well-nigh bankruptcy, Western Germany finished the decade of the 1950s with 80 per cent more reserves than Britain and the entire sterling area; yet the mark only had to finance 6 per cent of world trade, while sterling had to finance 33⅓ per cent of it and yield Britain a profit.

Devaluation No Remedy

By the middle of the 1950s the benefits of the devaluation of the pound in 1949 had been exhausted in export markets. Britain's competitors in these markets (especially the USA, Germany and Japan) had been gaining ground on her since 1950. The unfavourable effects of the devaluation inside the country were continuing. Inflation was uninterrupted. The thing that had caused devaluation to be necessary was now nourished by it. Britain could not hope to keep this up, and to hold her Commonwealth and sterling area friends in economic co-operation with her, if there were a danger that every two years or so, or with even accelerating frequency, her currency would be devalued, and so force devaluation on all of theirs. They could hardly be expected to go on earning balances in dollars and marks and other 'hard' currencies, and handing them over to the UK, in exchange for a pound which was becoming rapidly softer and softer in its purchasing power. Even less could they be expected to go on piling up and leaving in London those sterling balances, the proceeds of their toil and soil, in a currency which the British themselves were depreciating.

Among the sterling countries, the fifty-one million people of the British Isles—endowed by Nature only with skills, leadership, aptitudes, trainability, brains and wisdom—were the people with the highest standard of living. They therefore stood to lose most in material welfare from uninterrupted depreciation of the pound, its devaluation, and the break-up of the sterling area. That this danger existed can be gauged from two aspects of the 1956-57 version of the post-war sterling crises:

(a) the central gold and dollar reserve of the whole sterling area in London had sunk to danger-level; the amount of world trade and its value had risen, yet the reserves had fallen; this was because other members of the area than Britain (e.g. India) had overspent on imports, as well as being due to general distrust abroad of sterling's future in view of developments inside and outside Britain; and

(b) the distrust of the general trend inside Britain felt by foreigners persisted in spite of Britain's performance in maintaining her own balance of payments in credit with the rest of the world; foreigners looked back to 1947, 1949, 1951 and 1954 and wondered if Britain could ever stop inflation.

It followed that the first requirement for the safety of sterling— and of the welfare of the British people and their friends in the sterling area—was the repair of the economic foundations of their welfare. That could only be done by halting the long inflation, or at least by moderating it to a rate below that registered in America, Germany and elsewhere.

Halting inflation was the only sure and certain foundation for encouraging new long-term investment of new savings: savings induced by confidence in the future value of the pound; savings earned from increased productive efficiency of men and machines. These new savings were essential to finance the new investment programmes in Britain (and less industrialized sterling countries)

47

which were being loudly, widely and urgently demanded; in Britain to construct modern schools, hospitals, highways, railways, ports, ships and so forth; in economically less developed lands to raise agricultural productivity and to begin industrialization and diversification. To make such development projects possible it was vital to call a halt to the rate at which the purchasing power of the pound was falling, a rate sufficient to destroy half the currency's worth in one decade.

For these needs the actions—and inactions—of successive governments were useless. Inflation as a policy ran flatly counter to saving and to long-term investment in government bonds. Indeed, Socialist apologists for 'only a little', but a regular, inflation managed to inspire a major devaluation by 1949 and then as major an inflation after it as before it. (Mr—as he then was—Attlee's 'consequential measures' were announced in the autumn of 1949 but never taken.¹) So far did dislike of private property and saving take Socialist thinkers that even in the late 1950s some of them still advocated expropriation by deliberate inflation, *after* lulling savers and investors into a false sense of security by intermittent periods of stable prices. ('Securities' had in better days been the word for savings willingly lent to governments honouring their bonds.) This led one commentator to the following observation:

'There may be argument about the precise social and economic consequences of inflation, although no adult German, for example, will have the least doubt about them. But what can be said of the claim made by Mr Alan Day in the *Observer* (29 November, 1959), and apparently shared by other young economists, that "periods of stability" are "a good thing in that they suggest to some people that price stability has come to stay, so that confidence in the currency is restored"? This suggestion shows scant respect for the intelligence of the emerging masses. Will not a mature electorate see it as a confidence trick?'²

Redistribution by Taxation and Inflation
There was a fourth reason—not widely appreciated and even

¹ See author's article in *The Observer*, November 6, 1949, 'Inflation to Order'.
² See footnote on page 103 of *Not Unanimous: A Rival Verdict to Radcliffe's on Money*. London, Institute of Economic Affairs, 1960.

less publicized—why three quarters of the British people were able to raise their consumption, on average, by 30 per cent compared with before the war. In point of brutal fact, the 30 per cent increase in the consumption of these three quarters of the people by 1960 was taken, not so much from their own increased output or productivity, but largely from the incomes of the remaining one quarter of the population. This was inevitable if three quarters of the people were to consume 30 per cent more *out of an output available for consumption purposes only just over one-eighth bigger than in 1938-39.* Yet this increase in output *available for consumption* meant that insufficient was saved for all urgent capital demands to be met. So, inevitably, the consumption of the remaining quarter of the people was far lower than it was in 1939.

That might not have mattered, in justice or in politics, if those whose consumption had been compulsorily slashed by penal taxation and inflation had been all 'the rich'. But it was far from true that this luckless quarter were the rich and better-off who could afford it. Even before the war the better-off were never more than one-twentieth to one-tenth of the nation. In the postwar years, after high taxation, less than one-twentieth of the population could be called better-off. Yet one quarter of all the British people were consuming less after the war, on average, than before. Of course, a small minority of this quarter were 'the rich'. But the majority were all the old and retired, everybody living on a fixed income, lawyers, accountants, doctors and other professional people or unorganized workers who could not force up their income levels, civil servants, local government officers, managers in both State and private enterprises, technicians, technologists, and many workers of proven responsibility and skill— in fact, any household receiving, on average, over £1,000 a year in gross income in 1959. And in this context it should not be forgotten that with full employment there were on average *nearly two whole weekly pay-packets going into each household* in that three quarters of the populace covered by wages and lower salaries, who were now so much better-off than in 1939.

The one quarter therefore who were worse off were overwhelmingly the old, who deserved better of the nation, or the people on whom the nation's future as an industrial democracy depended. These were the people on whom were placed, almost exclusively, the material sacrifices demanded by the fighting of a war and by Britain's changed, debt-burdened position in an altered world. They had to make the sacrifices on behalf of the nation.

The other three quarters of the population were able to escape the overburdening and overstrain, the very inflation even, by pushing up their incomes not only to offset the depreciation of the pounds they earned, but also to race ahead of it and gain in power to consume. They were also the three quarters of the nation to whom, on balance, the new State welfare accorded most of its benefits. On average, their incomes outpaced the cost of living from 1954 onwards, so that their consumption of goods and services, their real (not money) income, continued to rise. Their gains were made throughout the decade and a half which followed the war and largely because of penal progressive taxation coupled with inflation. The remaining quarter of the British people bore the material losses, the reductions in real income.

Against that obvious prosperity of the mass of the British people, three quarters of them, there are thus a large number of costs to be weighed: the recurrent crises of overstrain, and of over-importing for consumption; the lags, lacks and shortfalls in the many overdue modernization programmes (like those which could have speeded transport); the disincentives to personal saving; the incentives to spending, to push up costs and pass them on (in higher prices) to the favoured three quarters of the nation —who were able to bear them anyway because, being organized, or influential as big voting groups, they could simultaneously push up, and win, their demands for more pay so long as governments continued to overspend and pump out new money.

Social Stresses and Strains

Such sacrifices and costs borne by only a quarter of the people were by their nature not the kind of costs to be felt by the mass, the majority, the three quarters. If they did not have a direct, tangible effect on those three quarters of the nation whose level of consumption was so much raised, they nevertheless were indirectly responsible for that malaise, that disquiet, which most people shared. That uneasiness was occasioned by a sense of insecurity, of uncertainty that the rising standards of life they had come to regard as a continuous phenomenon would in fact continue much longer, of disbelief in the future. It was thus through this doubt that the evils of inflation affected even those who for so long kept pace with, or even overtook, the upward movements of prices.

As this doubt lingered in their minds, anxiety grew at the constant, powerful pressure of the biggest, most organized group of British voters : the trade unions. By 1959 most of the electorate in Britain, including many of the trades unions' most loyal members, had come to fear the power which organized labour could exercise upon democratic governments. It was manifestly, after a decade and a half of its exercise, one of the biggest causes, if not the biggest single cause, of inflation as a policy : inflation determined, or acquiesced in, because the seeking and ensuring of sound money would have arrayed the biggest organized grouping of voters and income-demanders against any government of the day, and perhaps even against democracy itself. Therewith came acute bitterness, a sense of inequity and injustice, envy, and much hostility. Therewith, too, came the arbitrary altering of rewards, 'differentials' of different trades unions and their members, and social and industrial unrest. Thus within British democracy social tensions and political fissures were developed by inflation akin to those created in the ancient world and in other modern countries : tensions and fissures capable of undoing democratic society itself.

PART II

HOW?

CHAPTER 4

MONEY AND THE STATE

Modern industrial society can only run on money. The Russians found that out. Not even Communism can run a modern industrial system without money. A system reposing on exchange of goods and services for goods and services—barter—would be hopelessly slow, cumbrous and costly. 'Money is what money does.' What it does is measure the relative costs, selling prices, and values of all economic activities one against another: just as inches, pints or ounces measure the lengths, volumes or weights of things. But whereas these ordinary measures never vary because if they did nobody could be sure of anything, money units—shillings, marks, dollars—themselves vary in extraordinary ways.

An inch, a pint, an ounce is only an abstract idea. It only becomes a fact when attached to cloth, liquids, or solids. But a dollar, a pound sterling, a franc is not only an abstract idea. It is already a value: a 'value in exchange' in itself, a piece of 'purchasing power', a 'unit of currency', legal tender in any transaction for just so much of anything else. Trouble in people's thinking, and in public affairs, arises because all modern money includes credit: *i.e.* not only coin, banknotes, and cheques drawn on banks, but also *permits* from lenders to borrowers which give the latter *more* 'purchasing power'. A bank giving such a permit to a client to overdraw—to draw cheques (money) to buy more things over and above his stock of money at the time—is increasing the supply of money and credit (unless some former borrower at that moment is repaying a former credit of that amount somewhere). So is a trader who grants a customer a longer period of 'tick' in which to repay a trade debt. So is a government which, by borrowing from the banks, is spending more than its tax or other revenue and more than the proceeds of its sales of bonds to investors (for their savings). The more such credit is created on balance (*i.e.* over and above repayments of former credits) the more ordinary money will also be needed to do the extra work: more coin, banknotes, cheques, etc.

So if the total supply of *money and credit* in any period is expanding at a faster rate than the total supply of things to spend it on, there will be more and more monetary units of measure. The units of monetary measure will each diminish in purchasing power over goods. They will be getting smaller, as if inches were reduced to half-inches. Double the number of half-inches measures the same length of timber as a number of inches. The length of timber is the same. So, too, doubling the flow of money and credit in any period, while merely maintaining the supply of things to spend it on in the markets, will simply send holders of twice the amount of purchasing power into those markets to buy the same available things. More of some things will be wanted, the same amounts of others; more luxuries, hardly any more bread. But supplies of things are the same; so some things' prices will more than double, some prices won't rise much, some perhaps not at all. Yet the general, average, price level will be broadly double what it was as the doubled supply of money and credit goes round on offer, doing its buying work. And the whole pattern of production will be convulsed as more money bids more of certain things into production, out of *limited* resources.

Present and Future Things

If, as in primitive societies, only immediately consumable things (like simple food) were produced and placed on offer in markets, the problems of inflation would not be so complex. But modern industrial society is a form of social organization at which all the world for the first time in history is striving to arrive as fast as possible. And in industrialized societies more and more production, more employment, more machinery and buildings are *not* for immediately consumable things. They are for capital goods: things in durable use by consumers (houses, cars, home equipment, other gadgets) and by producers (factories, ports, railways, highways, mines, machines of all kinds, tools). To produce all this capital equipment for producers and consumers alike takes much time, many skills, specialization, and a lot of different kinds of manpower and machine-power. They are all in very limited supply, expandable only slowly.

Capital equipment *is* industrialism, in Russia as in America. Industrialization is the building-up and working of capital equipment. It is all the invested, frozen, congealed savings of some people somewhere, who have not spent all the money and credit they had available at the moment on immediately consumable things. Their savings—freely made in a democracy, either individually or collectively in the shape of business profits or insurance premiums—are invested in the equipment and production of *things for future uses.* To get a lot more savings very suddenly is difficult. Suddenly to boost monetary demand for those capital things by inflating is dangerous, for the savings and resources out of which they are made are limited. Their prices will rise formidably, and so therefore will demand for all these ingredients (including, of course, skilled labour). Employment of all resources will also therefore tend to become full, and if inflation persists over-full.

This distinction between immediately consumable things and things with uses in the future is crucial. It is mainly a difference between income and capital, spending and saving, present uses and future uses, work for present consumption and work for future uses and consumption. Industrialism, which is capitalism, depends on a balance between present spending and saving for the future. Its growth depends on a balance between *saving* out of presently available money and credit and *investing* that saving in things to be produced for future use. The economic growth of any society depends on how much of somebody's immediate purchasing power (money and credit) can be saved and invested in the increasing new forms of capital equipment, to expand output of all wanted things (whether for consumers or producers) in the future.

The investment of savings buys time. They finance the time, managerial and other human skills and know-how, the materials, fuel and power, transport, building space, and all other ingredients needed to make any tool or piece of capital equipment. The Stone Age cave-dwellers who kept a skilled flint-knapper and his family in meat and skins and cave-room to furnish the best weapons for the chase were saving immediately available meat and skins and cave-room and investing them in a tools factory and in the payment of wages to its skilled labour. They were increasing their own hunting efficiency, *i.e.* their standard of living, by investment in new and better capital equipment. They were financing (investing savings in) time, know-how, capital (a factory) and labour for future improvements.

Now if a democratic society needs new tools and productive capital equipment, it must make it worth some savers' while—*all* the while, all the time required to make them—not to spend immediately available purchasing power (whether the latter is money and credit or mammoth-tusks) merely for immediate consumption. This buying of time and the buying of present resources of all kinds, to convert them into new things with future uses, is investment. Borrowing savings, investing someone's present purchasing power in a conversion job over a period of time, has its cost—which is the rate of interest paid to the saver. The borrower pays interest for the time during which he borrows another's purchasing power. Interest is calculated at so many units per hundred units borrowed, per year of the loan: 6 per cent per annum = £6 or $6 every year per £100 or $100 of someone else's money and credit. The interest rate rises the longer the time, for in a longer time risks increase, and other opportunities to spend which the lender could have taken will have to be given up by him. If the borrower succeeds in his capital-employing, and perhaps capital-producing, venture, he will make a *profit* (over and above all costs, including the interest he pays) out of which he will pay himself a 'dividend on enterprise': the reward for his own risk of losing everything. He will also, if profits are big enough, 'plough back' some into the venture and so provide it with new capital out of its own new savings, either for use or to repay the original capital sum which was borrowed. In either case ploughed-back profits are new savings.

Time—present and future, spending or saving, long and short-term—is at the heart of saving and investment, at the heart of all building-up of capital, and therefore at the heart of capitalistic industrialism and industrial capitalism (whether Russian or American).

Inflation, Investment and Profits

Accordingly it is imperative that units of purchasing power saved and invested at present prices should yield interest, as the time of the loan or investment rolls by, at exactly the fixed annual rate calculated by lenders and borrowers when they contracted, and in units of the same purchasing power.

But inflation multiplies the units of purchasing power more than the things they are spent on. Inflation therefore makes all money costs and prices go up during the life of the loan or investment. So if the lender agreed in 1960 to invest £100 of savings for ten years at 6 per cent and by 1970 the price level had doubled, he would get back his *nominal or face-value* capital of £100 by 1970; but it would only buy what £50 bought in 1960. He would have lost one-half of his *real* capital: one-half of its original purchasing power over real goods. Worse, he would not even have received in the ten years the *real* 6 per cent he had bargained for. Only the £6 interest received for that first year by the end of 1960 would have had the full 1960 purchasing power. In 1961, 1962, 1963 and so on till the end of 1969, each year's *fixed* interest of £6 on the £100 of capital invested would buy less than the first £6 received in 1960. And the last £6 of interest received in 1969 would only buy one-half of the things which the first £6 had bought a decade earlier.

So the borrower would get £100 worth of *real capital* (*i.e.* things, resources, goods and services) from the saver or lender in 1960. But instead of paying a *real* 6 per cent rate of interest each year for ten years on this original loan of 1960's purchasing power, he would be paying a lower and lower *real* rate of interest year after year, as money and credit are inflated and the prices of things rise. And at the end of 1969 and of the term of the fixed-interest loan, he would be able to repay the original saver and lender with half the purchasing power of the original loan, half the amount of 1960 goods and services. That is why inflation always works against long-term lending at fixed interest, and in favour of 'equities' which must 'share' in the rising inflationary profits from rising prices.

Meanwhile the borrower would have at once converted the loan in 1960 into *real* resources—wages, materials, factory space, fuel and power, etc.—and used these over and over again in the ten years. He would have been buying them and converting them into end-products easily sold at rising prices because of the inflation. So the borrower would be buying-in his resources at one price level, converting them, and selling the products later on at a slightly higher level, thus making not only a normal profit but also a continuous inflationary profit, a 'windfall profit', an uncovenanted benefit in extra money-receipts over money-costs.

Moreover, this is a profit element bearing no relation to the efficiency of the enterprise. It comes from without, from inflation of the customers' purchasing power. That is why inflation always works in favour of ordinary, risk-bearing, equity shares, risk capital. The investor of savings in such equity capital enjoys the protection of a built-in 'hedge' against inflation, as long as the inflating government does not tax away *all* those inflationary profits. Either the businessman-borrower—company, farmer, offerer of services, trader—can go on making inflationary profits easily year by year, or he can sell out his business to others who by then will want to acquire a 'hedge' against the inflation. In the latter case he will of course make a capital profit which (at least in many countries, including Britain) is not taxable. He will have sold a business valued at, say, £1,000 in 1960 for £1,500 or even £2,000 by 1965 or so.

This capital value of the business will in fact tend to rise *faster* than the rate at which the money loses its purchasing power. For everybody will soon be aware of the dangers of fixed-interest investments in the inflation. They will be vying with each other to buy businesses, equity shares, land or real estate, even antiques, old masters and even young masters, or anything else offering a built-in 'hedge' against the continuous rise in the price level, because its price is likely to rise with that level. The supply of such investments is always limited. It will become more strictly limited, and the prices of such investments will soar disproportionately higher, as everyone bids for the relatively few coming on to the various investment and capital markets.

Thus inflation brings uncovenanted profits and capital gains which bear little relation to efficiency, competitiveness, or technical progress. On the contrary, it tends to keep in existence—in a spuriously profitable existence—enterprises (private or State-owned) which in the course of technical progress, of economical use of savings and other resources, and of competitive efficiency to achieve more rapid economic growth, would have gone out of production. The resources they still use would have been more profitably used for everyone—workers, producers, consumers, the

State—in other ways, had not the inflationary veil been cast over their real costs of operation.

Time and Value

Time is of the essence of the inflation problem. When the government of a modern industrial, and therefore highly complex, society deliberately depreciates the purchasing power of its currency as it goes along—or lazily acquiesces in its loss of purchasing power by allowing the supply of it to expand faster than national production and productivity—the units of measurement for all values will not only depreciate. They will depreciate more and more through time. They will have greater purchasing power over the bulk of immediately purchasable consumers' goods and services coming on to markets, but less over the smaller (but crucial, more costly, and much longer-to-make) supply of capital goods required for the future. Money now and real goods now will be worth more than money to come or property to come.

Prices will rise, but not all to the same extent or in the same degree. According to the degree or rate of inflation, all investment will be diverted first from low to high fixed-interest at long-term, then from long-term fixed-interest to short-term fixed-interest or wholly risk-bearing investment (equity investment), and finally away from investment in future production altogether. If inflation becomes breakneck, no one will save or invest in normal production for the future. People will not hold money. They will spend frantically, to get real goods. Goods will become measures of value themselves, one being valued in terms of another in the primitive exchange system of barter, as society's monetary measure breaks down. Society will revert to a pre-credit, pre-monetary stage, which will render capitalistic and industrial production, banking, credit and trade impossible.

The governor and pivot of the capitalistic, industrial system is thus reliability of the measure of values through a reasonable time to come. It is the dependability of the currency as a measure and medium for the ever-increasing and more complicated exchanges and transactions in industrial society. These are not only between buyers and sellers of things in the present, but to an increasing extent also between present purchasing power (savings) and future purchasing power (future yields on investment).

Of course, the *real* values always remain, whether in American or in Russian society: the tons of this, freight-miles of that, gallons, yards, man-hours of work, machine-hours of work, cubic feet of work-space in buildings, kilowatts or gallons of fuel and power, and so on. These are all ingredients of one thing or another produced, offered, and wanted. But over them all, in Russia and America, is spread the veil of money values giving them all their relative magnitudes in prices. Thus monetary units measure the comparative values of all these real things, price their qualities one against another, and cost all operations, whether for delivery in the present or in the future.

If the authorities in a progressively industrializing society allow these measuring units of all values themselves to alter (by raising the proportion between the supply of money or credit and that of things) the natural variations through time between the values of different things in terms of each other will be altered. New relationships will be set up, not only between the real values of things but between present and future. Wheat normally cheapens through bumper harvests, equipment cheapens through new inventions, expert human skills get dearer because of longer training. But these natural variations between *real* values will be veiled and artificially distorted by an overall variation downwards in the measuring rod, the value of the monetary unit itself. More money will be used for one thing, less for another; *not the same proportion more will be used for each.* Businesses, the State itself, trade unionists, managers, farmers—some of these will get more of the extra money, some less. The total purchasing power of some of them will rise, of others fall. So production of different things will become as distorted as incomes, taxes, pensions, etc., and their real purchasing power.

Finally, distortion will occur between present spending and saving, between consumption and investment, and between lending at moderate rates of fixed interest for medium and long terms and instead not lending at all, or lending at high rates for short periods only, or speculation in increasing numbers of risk-bearing ventures (equities) or commodities, works of art, land, real estate, etc. Consumption and speculation and quick-turnover ventures are thus stimulated by inflation—the more so the more rapid the inflation—at the expense of long-term investment in normal, enduring, productive capital. Inflation thus engenders confusion of all values, hectic velocity of money and dealings and all other economic activities, and innumerable quick unreliabilities in place of long-term dependabilities.

Steady growth is hampered. The quickest 'turns' on depreciating money are eagerly sought. And everyone soon becomes aware of an undesirable hecticness in the nation's economic life, an unnatural monetary fever. It is too easily and too often mistaken for real and rapid progress in the nation's wellbeing, whereas it is really a hectic boost to present consumption, at the cost of a slower growth in wellbeing than would have been possible on sound money. A lot of purchasing power which would have been saved and invested in durable, productive innovations is dissipated in consumption or in unproductive 'hedges' and hoards.

When this awareness of inflation, of preference for present goods over future goods, becomes general, democratic governments have desperate recourse to State controls and permits over the *real* things, over the normal businesses, jobs, and other economic activities of their citizens. They try to stop the present hectic rush to get rid of depreciating money. They attempt by cooling the thermometer to cure the patient's fever. They attack only the symptoms, not the disease which still proceeds. And so an inflating industrial democracy hampers its own growth, jeopardizes its future, and eventually undemocratizes itself. The inflating democracy inflates democracy away.

Money and the State

The power over, and decisions about, the supply of all kinds of money—cash, notes, bank deposits (bank credit), trade credit, government bills and other short-term IOUs—are in all nations ultimately the responsibility of governments. To allow it to be otherwise would be to go back to the days of private coining, private banknotes, and (of course) very private counterfeiting.

With the vast growth of the modern State's powers over everyone and everything, that State has to raise vast funds to finance both the *current*, day-to-day costs of the State machine and bureaucracy, and the longer-run *capital* projects now undertaken by State authorities, boards and agencies (*e.g.* in Britain, France, Sweden and other 'mixed' economies, the coalmines, railways, gas and electricity services, housing, highways, etc.).

Most of the day-to-day needs of the State are met from taxes. Such current needs include subsidies for State welfare, farmers, etc, the cost of defence, and the cost of running the National Debt (paying the interest, and repaying the principal when due, of all moneys lent in the past to the Government in exchange for its long-term 'gilt-edged' IOUs or bonds and its short-term IOUs or bills), and the cost of all Government offices, services and staffs at home and abroad. The taxes to defray all these day-to-day State expenses are raised through the yearly Budgets.

If they bring in more than goes out, there is a Budget surplus; if less, there is a Budget deficit. The surplus mops up taxpayers' money and puts it at the State's disposal. If the State then spends it—on anything—out it goes again into circulation to pay firms and people who have worked for the State; and so the surplus disappears. If the States does not spend a Budget surplus, but cancels some of its own paper IOUs with it (reduces the National Debt), the nation's supply of money and credit is cut down. It is deflating to that extent, because the stream of goods and services continues (for at least a time) to flow in the same volume, while the parallel stream of money to be spent on that volume of goods and services dwindles a little. Less money; more goods; prices tend to fall if the deflation goes on. Later on awkward decisions have to be taken by producers of goods and services, as selling prices fall and profits fall with them. Weak producers, producers 'at the margin' who were only just making a profit before, will now make a loss and won't be able to go on doing so for very long. So a series of Budget surpluses which are not spent by the Government is much the same as a credit squeeze in its effects.

But if there is a Budget deficit—i.e. if the State spends *more* than it gets in taxes—it must pay its accounts with more money than it is collecting. It therefore borrows from its bankers, who create credit for it, just as a bank manager gives a firm or a private person an overdraft. But there is a great difference between the State's short-term borrowings of bank credit and a company's or an individual's. The State's short-term IOUs handed to its bankers *are* money. They swell the banking system's reserves because they are short-term obligations of the Government and can pass from bank to bank as money. They are reckoned money, because they are reckoned 'as safe as the Bank of England' or as safe as 'gilt-edged'. So when the State finances its own overspending by this means, when it finances a Budget deficit this way, it is inflating the supply of money just as definitely as if it had printed that amount of new banknotes and pushed them into circulation by paying its due accounts and the wages and salaries of civil servants with them.[1]

There is, however, the second account of the State: not its current day-to-day spending, but its long-term or *capital* account as abovementioned. For that, the State has to raise funds which are going to be locked up for a long time in schools, hospitals, harbours, housing, railways, coalmines, power stations, gas grids, and all the other valuable and durable capital apparatus of the modern State. (Armaments and one or two less important but durable things are by tradition covered in the day-to-day current accounts of the yearly Budget.) These durable assets of the State should yield substantial services to individual and corporate citizens through the years to come. To get the money to make them, the State should borrow at long-term. That is, the State sells its own long-term IOUs, called 'gilt-edged' or Government long-term bonds, to any of its own individual and corporate citizens and foreigners who will buy them at the prices and long-term rates of interest the State must accept.

The State's Tendency to Inflate

There are thus two main accounts which the modern industrial State must watch all the time: the level of its current (day-to-day) account, and the level of its capital (long-term) account. It can raise more taxes than it needs for its *current* account—*i.e.* create a Budget surplus—and then spend exactly that surplus on its *capital* programme. In that case, to cover its whole capital programme, it will not need to offer as many new long-term 'gilt-edged' Government bonds in the capital market. The savings of companies (profits) and of individuals (*e.g.* insurance premiums) flowing into that market for long-term investment will then tend to find fewer outlets. That will tend to lower the long-term rate of interest for borrowing, which in turn will stimulate businesses and other private and public enterprises to borrow and undertake long-term projects to expand productive capital equipment.

But if the State runs a Budget deficit on its current account, or merely balances its current account, yet undertakes on its long-term capital account *more* than it can (or is willing to) finance by selling long-term Government bonds in the market, it will be

[1] See Chapter 5, p. 85.

forced to create credit for itself by the short-term Government IOU method described above. It will then be 'borrowing short' to 'invest long'. It will be overspending *on both accounts added together* at the same time. This wouldn't matter if, to match it exactly, private firms and individuals were willing to save—*i.e.* not to spend so much—and lend to the State at long-term. But they won't be prepared to do this if money is losing its purchasing power already; and certainly not for only moderate rates of fixed interest.

The State will therefore be creating more money than hitherto existed, so that it shall get first cut at the country's existing resources of men, materials and machines. It will be doing this in order to carry out its own spending programmes, before its individual and corporate citizens can buy enough of those same national resources to carry out theirs. The stream of money will immediately swell, but the stream of goods and services—of resources—won't. So bidders will contend with more money for the same volume of resources. The bidder who bids most will get first cut. The State always gets first cut, for it enjoys the prime priority of making new money. And as this inflation of the currency works its way through the country's existing supplies of men's work, of materials and of machine-capacity, the prices of all these resources begin to go up, as the bidders who can afford more outbid those who can't.

The only exception to this way of sparking-off and continuing an inflation is when a nation is in an economic depression or slump, *i.e.* when there are pools of *unemployed* resources—men, materials and machines—lying idly around. Then, the creation of new purchasing power by the State can absorb the unemployed resources, *up to the level of 'full employment' of all resources.* But if the creation of new money continues beyond that level—if the expansion of credit causes a boom, the State's spending and private enterprises' spending now competing for resources which cannot be expanded quickly enough—then nothing can stop the whole price-level moving up and up, as bidders contend with more money for relatively scarcer resources. Orders pile up, delivery dates extend, wage demands soar, profits increase. Full employment rapidly becomes over-full employment.

There are only two possible results to such a boom. First a collapse can occur due to prices soaring beyond some buyers' reach (generally foreigners' reach, as prices of the country's exports outstrip those quoted by competitors). This brings a sorry relief in the shape of some *unemployed* resources somewhere and a consequent distressing fall in prices, profits and production. Resources are made available again in an unpleasant way. Or, secondly, careful corrective measures by the State will have to be taken to trim State and private spending, so that the flow of money and credit comes once more into balance with the flow of the country's currently available goods and services (resources). No control of prices can resolve this dilemma.

Right Way or Primrose Way?

It is therefore inescapably the duty of the modern industrial State, as it certainly lies solely within its power, to guard against the twin causes of inflation: first, the combined overspending on current and capital accounts by the State, as compared with the funds the State is subtracting (by taxes and borrowing) from its citizens' flow of purchasing power; and secondly, the ordering of its own programmes and those of the nation, through its monetary powers, so that total monetary demands run ahead of the nation's total real resources. If the State does not avoid and avert these two threats to a sound, reliable currency, it will very soon find its own long-term bonds refused in the market. Inflation will be boosting money around faster and faster, as prices rise, and as bidders (the State's boards and agencies included) hurriedly try to get out of depreciating money into the goods and services which are coming forward more slowly than the stream of money. Profits, on paper, rise quickly. 'The velocity of circulation' of money rises. A boom is on. No one will lend at long-term to the State when profits are rising, prices are rising, money is losing its purchasing power, and long-term interest rates over the years do not match the money's loss of its face value.

The standing temptation to States in such inflationary predicaments is to put out still *more* money and credit, to make sure that the State's agencies can buy what they want first. So inflation merrily proceeds. But soon the State and its agencies find they can only 'borrow short', since few lenders will lend their savings at modest rates of fixed interest for years to come. As the State authorities borrow more and more 'short' to finance their over-ambitious 'long' programmes—and, soon, to repay old long-term bonds falling due—the huge modern National Debts become composed, more and more, first of medium-term and finally of shorter-term Government obligations. National Debts thus tend, in uninterrupted inflations, to become 'monetized': *i.e.* they tend to become composed more and more of short-term Government paper which acts as money; which indeed is money within the banking system. And so the inflation feeds its own furnaces, pumping more and more government bills (short-term reserves) into the banks, and enabling them to extend more and more credit (bank money). The result, if inflation is not arrested, is as sure a collapse of the country's currency this way as if the State had simply gone on printing more and more banknotes.[1]

Not the least of inflation's paradoxes is that its inevitable periodic crises compel inflating governments to produce, despite themselves, the very situations from which they hoped to escape by inflating. In such 'crises of confidence' they are compelled, often in abrupt last-minute panic, to raise taxation, clap on controls, and launch 'dear-money' policies which can only suddenly safeguard the currency by making money and credit far more difficult to get, and far dearer if got, than would ever have been necessary if sound money had been maintained all along. Such last-minute, desperate correctives of inflationary crises can only 'correct' by forcing—at long last—some unemployment of men and machines, of labour and capital, upon the society. This is the very situation from which inflation is vulgarly supposed to save a society. No inflation at all is a better recipe for steady growth. It only involves such transitional unemployment of men and machines as is indicated by independent, automatic, neutral indicators, without regular crises and panics.

[1] See Chapter 5, p. 87.

THE NATURE OF INFLATION

Inflation, like sentiment, is a word capable of two meanings: one coloured, one colourless. Both meanings refer to a state of affairs in which money becomes relatively more common than the things on which money can be spent at ruling market prices.

The colourless meaning of inflation refers to the condition of a country when the general price level—the average of all prices—goes on rising from year to year over a lengthy period. That is, the purchasing power of its money is falling. Its currency is depreciating as against the value of goods and services. Such a condition can come about from many causes. Wars and pestilences cause it, like the Black Death of 1348 or the World Wars of 1914-18 and 1939-45, which destroyed people, productive capital, and their products but left the same, or greater, amounts of money in circulation. Interruption of normal supplies of goods and services can cause inflation, as in a besieged city or beleaguered country—Paris in 1870-71, Britain in the World Wars—when the supply of money stays up or even rises farther, while the supply of goods on which to spend it is reduced.

New discoveries and exploitation of gold and silver deposits can cause it, as in the case of the sixteenth-century American dominions of Spain, and of Californian, South African and Australian gold last century. New financial methods can cause inflation, like the printing and use of banknotes, or the use of bank credit over and above the money value of the coin and bullion (gold and silver) in the banks—as in Britain, Holland, and other advanced countries between 1660 and today. All of these causes, however, operate accidentally or incidentally upon the supply of money in question.

The coloured meaning of inflation, on the other hand, refers to the condition of a country when the continuous rise in its general price level—the depreciation of its currency, the loss of its money's purchasing power—stems directly from *deliberate* expansion of the flow of money and credit by the country's financial authorities, at a faster rate than the flow of things on which money and credit can be spent. This cause of inflation is political. It is a deliberate act of policy whether it is positively willed by the monetary authorities, or merely negatively permitted by them because they cannot, do not want to, or fear to, stop it. Inflation as an act of policy is never incidental or accidental. It never operates upon the supply of money and credit from outside—like wars, plagues, new supplies of monetary gold, interrupted communications, or new methods of financing. The more modern, usual, familiar, and by now derogatory meaning of the word inflation is this second coloured meaning. It is that which is used when the relatively more rapid supply of money than of the things on which it can be spent at ruling market prices is due to an act of policy by the monetary authorities. It is that political meaning of inflation with which this book is concerned.

Both kinds of inflation, both rises in the general price level which result from 'more money chasing the same amount of things', are diminished, modified or offset by expansion in the flow of things for sale. When famine is overcome by a new bumper harvest, prices fall. ('Here's a farmer that hanged himself on the expectation of plenty.'[1]) Populations increase after plagues or wars. War damage is made good. Shortages are overcome by investment of new savings in new productive capital equipment. The application of new scientific techniques makes two blades of grass grow where one grew before, and a new machine or method turns out more than the old one which it replaces. Human skills increase and multiply. Communications improve and swell the volume of things and services exchanged by trading. So the expanded flow of goods and services offered for sale in the markets tends to catch up with, and match, the expanded flow of money offered in those markets, and to offset inflation.

Expansion of the supply of money and credit thus carries within it a moderating influence—as long as it is kept in step with expansion of the supply of goods and services. Even if the

[1] Macbeth, II, 3.

year-to-year rise in the general price level goes on at something between 1 and 2 per cent, individuals and companies will—for a time—still save and invest in new productive capacity which raises productivity and offsets inflationary effects; will still lend or borrow; will still abstain from spending their current incomes or profits up to the hilt; will still look to a future in which money will still have some purchasing power, some value, and therefore some reliability as a measure of all other costs and values and as a store of wealth. In that case the new machines and productive capacity made possible by the new savings and investments will continuously come into operation. So will the applications of new techniques and methods, and the work and skills of new men and women as population grows. Output of goods and services will rise to match the earlier inflationary rise in the flow of money, and the bigger flow of goods and services to markets will therefore tend to diminish or control the inflation of all prices in those markets.

Long Run and Short Run

The movement of the general price level in a country through a fair period of years is therefore the outcome of a shifting relationship between two flows: the flow of the money offered in markets for goods and services, and that of the goods and services into those markets in exchange for the money. If the flow of money into markets expands in that period more than the flow of all things on which it can be spent, inflation of prices, and therefore depreciation of the currency, follows. The purchasing power of money falls. If the converse happens, and the flow of goods and services offered in markets expands in the period more than the flow of money, deflation of prices, and therefore appreciation of the currency, follows. The purchasing power of money then increases.

According as one or the other, or neither inflation nor deflation, occurs, so will all income-receivers—individuals, companies, institutions, the State itself—decide whether to spend all their incomes, save some or much or little or none, borrow or lend at short or long term, incur or reduce debts, invest in new productive capacity for a long time or just 'stay liquid' with ready cash available and so 'buy time'. All these possible actions depend upon their actors' attitudes to money's worth, to the trend of prices, and therefore to the trend in the real purchasing power of money.

Few people realize how important in economic affairs are the views taken of the trend in the value of money by potential savers and investors, both individual and institutional. Their present view of the economic future; their comparisons of the worthwhileness of present spending on goods on the one hand, and of the saving and investing for a possible greater gain in the future on the other hand; their belief or disbelief in a continuation of economic growth at past and present rates or of inflation or deflation—all these attitudes elbow and jostle each other in the various markets for money, credit and capital. They swell or shrink supplies of each kind of purchasing power, and they overflow or fail to come up to the demands for each.

The various rates of interest react and are determined for varying periods accordingly: rates for long-term loans to match the volume of long-term investment in such big and durable capital goods as houses, factories, heavy machinery and installations, port equipment, schools, etc.; and rates for shorter-term loans to match individuals' and businesses' needs of day-to-day working capital, 'tide-over' credits, bank overdrafts, hire purchase advances, trade credit, etc.

All such financing of long-term and short-term needs is a recurrent, day-by-day necessity in a complex, modern, industrial society. The various rates of interest not only measure and reflect the varying pressures of potential borrowers' needs for finance and of potential savers' desires to invest. They also measure and reflect the worthwhileness of spending on goods immediately as against saving and investing *at all* (either at long or short term), and the worthwhileness of 'staying liquid' (*i.e.* not spending on goods immediately—saving, but *not* investing in anything for the moment) or investing only for a short term (*e.g.* in a building society, a savings bank, a bank deposit, a Government three-months' bill, etc.) instead of for a term of many years.

Thus the degree, duration, and rate of an inflation create in the minds of potential borrowers and savers, whether individuals or businesses, varying attitudes to the spending and saving of their existing money, their current purchasing power. If that current money, that currency, has been and is still losing its purchasing power at a fast rate due to a rapid inflation, it will be harder to get people to tie up savings for years at fixed interest rates. Businesses will want more and more money as all wages and other costs rise—so will Governments—both to pay for fixed, long-term, capital assets (like buildings) and for day-to-day working capital (as wages and other costs and prices go on rising). But savers will not be so keen on saving and investing, unless they get a 'share' in businesses: a 'hedge' against depreciation; an 'equity' which will rise in value, and in yield of dividend, as inflation goes on. Since governments do not borrow by issuing shares—only by issuing IOUs at fixed interest rates—the financing of governments' needs in an inflation becomes increasingly short-term and difficult; and business 'equities' are preferred to govern-ments' fixed-interest bonds. All rates of fixed interest rise. All dividend yields fall, as savers rush to buy business 'equities' as 'hedges' against currency depreciation, and so push up their prices on stock markets. As the prices of these ordinary shares rise, their existing rates of dividend show smaller and smaller returns or yields on the rising prices which have to be paid for them. There is a boom in ordinary shares, a slump in the price of Government bonds ('gilt-edged') and other fixed interest securities. This in-flationary pattern has been repeated in the economic texture of one industrial democracy after another during the past generation of war and its aftermath.

The Inflationary Dilemma
The argument against inflation as a policy in a democracy rests upon two counts: first, that such inflation arbitrarily alters all demand and supply, and all values, without reference to economy or efficiency—which is an economic count; and secondly, that it arbitrarily alters all legal and other social rela-tionships reared on the stability and continuity of such values—which is a sociological count. If it were possible precisely to fore-tell at any moment just what effects a given amount of inflation would produce in any given society, these two counts might fail, and the argument against inflation might fall to the ground.

Apologists for 'only a little one' might then point out, with some rough social justice, that a deliberately modest but steady and regular inflation would become absorbed into the daily *data* of a democracy: that it would be discounted in advance in all calculations; would become as taken for granted as the level of income tax or turnover tax or companies' profits tax; and would therefore make no *real* differences or alterations to anyone or anything. But that would be to misconceive the whole point of inflation *as a policy*. As soon as an entire society accepts a given rate of inflation as a *datum* and discounts its effect in advance in all calculations of value, the government—the inflating authority which gets the prior benefits of inflation—must step up its rate, in order to secure such prior benefits of fresh inflation over and above what the entire society expected and evaluated in advance.

Like a baby, 'only a little one' quickly becomes a big one. If it were not so, society would indeed adjust to the expected rate. The government would then quickly lose any continuous gain or benefit from a regular, steady rate of inflation. Equally quickly, it would find itself again facing all the awkward dilemmas and decisions from which it had run away by inflating in the first place. So any inflation *as a policy* must grow by feeding on itself, on its own effects. To get inflationary advantages over everyone else in the society *as a set policy*, a government must inflate more and more. This cumulative, compounding nature of inflation compels inflating democratic governments to place more and more compulsory controls on the individual and corporate life and business of their citizens. Thus to secure inflationary benefits for the State as a policy a democracy tends to undo itself.

Economic knowledge and analysis are nowhere within sight of being able to foretell with any accuracy what the effects of a given degree of inflation will be. They can tell very roughly what will follow, but only in the broadest outline. Even then, the given degree of inflation must continue steadily for a fair time. One 'shot in the arm' will not have the same effects all through a social organism that continuous, increasing doses will have. The effects of 'one shot', once and for all, are hard enough to prophesy; but they can be gauged—as when young John Maynard Keynes told his mother he could double the length of every shopping queue in England simply by slipping an extra £5 note into every pay-packet on one Friday only. When governments of democracies—or any others—have recourse to inflation it is almost always an act of despair. It is seldom, if ever, 'one shot' once and for all. The effects of such deliberate, steady, continuous, compounding inflation are easier to foretell, but even then only in the broadest of outlines.

What Inflation Does

It is unnecessary here to do more than describe such outlines. First, all contractual claimants to fixed sums in the future are penalized the longer and the more rapidly inflation goes on; but workers at all levels of income can raise their money incomes. Those organized in trade unions or professional bodies or pressure groups can do so more easily than those not so organized. But the longer and more rapidly inflation goes on, the higher go all earned incomes in the existing brackets of income tax and sur-tax; so inflation takes more in tax from the better-paid, the more responsible producers. So, too, the State Treasury has a vested interest in a long or rapid inflation because it automatically spells 'buoyancy of the revenue'. Just leaving income taxes, sur-tax, and profits taxes where they are must result in higher tax yields, as the rising incomes in depreciating money push their recipients into the higher brackets of 'progressive taxation'.

In Britain in 1949 scarcely any ordinary weekly wage-earner could have imagined ever becoming liable to sur-tax, which begins —as forty years ago—at £2,000 p.a. But in 1959 quite a number of such workers were already paying it. And by 1969, if inflation were to proceed as in 1949 to 1959, one-third of all weekly wage-earners would be sur-tax payers. Consequently the course of inflation in democracies with 'progressive taxation' (and what democracies are without it?) is (a) increasingly to penalize responsibility and good management, (b) progressively to advantage the State's tax revenue, thus giving it an automatic 'hedge' against inflation, (c) relatively to benefit, and therefore to stimulate demands from, the best-organized pressure groups, and (d) to advantage the lower income-earners whose *money* incomes can rise farthest before getting into brackets of 'progressive taxation' where heavy income tax becomes payable.

Secondly, inflation therefore penalizes—like a secret, increasing tax—all claimants to fixed money incomes in the future: all pensioners, holders of insurance policies without any rights to 'with profits' bonuses, holders of *all* fixed-interest securities at medium or long-term (*e.g.* government bonds, industrial debentures, simple preference shares), landlords of real estates leased for medium or long terms at fixed money rents, recipients of annuities bought by lump-sum down-payments earlier, owners of patents or copyrights or other 'know-how' who have granted

75

royalties or licences at fixed money fees for medium or long terms, and beneficiaries of trusts, covenants, and other funds, the money income from which depends on fixed-interest securities of any kind.

The social tensions and stresses set up by inflation between all such claimants to fixed money incomes and all other income-receivers in a democracy are well known since 1918. Each government tries to alleviate them in its own way by granting 'reliefs': raising the State's old-age pension rates, for instance (but not privately-secured pension rates). But this leads not only to fresh tensions and injustices. It also leads opposition political parties to bid for the votes of the social groupings most aggrieved by the inflation: *i.e.* mainly those which are unproductive (the retired, dependent, or sick) and/or those hitherto unorganized. Thereupon new social organisms arise embodying those suffering most from inflation, organized for party-political as much as economic or equitable purposes.

The result is generally to import into democratic politics, by an inflation conceived as a policy to *avoid* awkward social decisions, such a doubly awkward set of dilemmas as would never have been willingly or wittingly incurred at the outset, had the government and its advisers only known what lay in the infla-tionary wind. Should the government be outbid for votes and change hands in the ensuing whirlwind, the incoming party will probably run away from such doubly awkward dilemmas by having recourse to further inflation, rendering them quadruply awkward. Thus the process of undoing democracy—politically, economically, socially—proceeds cumulatively.

Thirdly, however, inflation confers a 'hedge' or an outright capital profit on all holders of liquid capital funds, of movable assets like ordinary 'equity' shares, of freehold farms or houses in their own occupation, or of anything else *immediately* saleable or usable in any business sense. As the purchasing power of money depreciates, people and businesses 'get out of' money and 'get into' *real* values: *i.e.* they get rid of money, and of any rights to receive fixed sums of it in the future, and rush instead to acquire titles to a share in any economic activity which (like organized workers) can push up its prices to cover its rising money costs. So down go the prices of all titles to fixed money incomes in the future, and up go those of all titles to future money incomes which can rise with the rising money value of trade and its profits. Up also go the prices of any durable object in general demand—a house, a genuine work of art, a diamond necklace—the supply of which is limited or difficult to expand quickly; for people rush to acquire such 'real values' in exchange for their increasing amounts of depreciating money.

Inflation against Society

These variable social effects of inflation interact. They are not independent variables. They are interdependent. People or associations entitled to fixed money incomes have their standards of life forcibly cut. They are forced to sell capital if they own it. Those who can push up their incomes in inflation, despite their liabilities to heavier income tax and sur-tax—e.g. those who are not yet in the highest income brackets, or those who can make even bigger trade profits, after tax, than the rise in money costs would warrant—buy the capital of those forced to sell it.

Most businesses are made highly profitable in paper money by inflation: they can pay their taxes—even if governments raise them, though they do not need to because of the abovementioned 'buoyancy of the revenue'—and all their rising money costs, yet 'plough-back' substantial net profits, and pay good dividends to shareholders. Other businesses and trades, especially those dependent on exports, may be badly hit; so may be their employees and shareholders. The interests of the old and retired are set against those of the young or middle-aged. Those of the unproductive are set against those of the productive. Those of the prudent 'truster'[1] who endowed trustees with his savings at fixed interest for long term in favour of beneficiaries in the future, and those of his beneficiaries too, are set against those of the quick 'in and out' operators who make virtue and profit out of *not* holding on to any money. The interests of all who save, contribute, build, and create for a long-term future are set against those dependent for profit on the highest 'velocity of circulation' of money. No one can trust money or government. Society and its once firm institutions begin to flounder in deepening flux.

So criticism of a policy of inflation from the social standpoint is not difficult. There can be no justice or equity in a *democratic* governmental policy which deliberately and arbitrarily injures

[1] *cestui que trust* is the legal term.

77

owners of one kind of savings and investment for the future (at fixed interest) and favours another (equities), which alters the terms of all contracts and other legal arrangements for property rights in the future, which does such things without public justification and explanation, and at arbitrary but secret rates of tax. The ensuing sense of injustice in many injured groupings of the society, the ensuing social stresses and tensions, rise with formidable, explosive force, the faster and farther the inflation goes.

The greatest single factor responsible for the rise of the Nazi movement to supreme power between 1923 and 1933 was the inflation deliberately pursued by the first democratic governments of the Weimar Republic. It created social tensions and discontents among the modest property-owners which Hitler and his helpers were easily able to capitalize. Much the same social tension followed deliberate inflations in Italy and Spain between the two world wars. In more recent times we have witnessed the foundering of the Fourth democratic French Republic and its supersession by a régime half-authoritarian, half-monarchical, in which parliament and representative government are reduced to symbols. The political systems supervening on democracies which have undone themselves by policies of inflation can better cope with the inflation and its effects, as now in France. But they generally do not. That does not invalidate the criticism of inflation from the social standpoint. Once done, the harm to social and political solidarity by a democracy's arbitrary alteration in all property rights is hard to undo.

Inflation against Economy

Criticism of a policy of inflation from the economic standpoint is even easier. Inflation causes an arbitrary 'windfall' distribution of inflationary profits, divorced from productive efficiency or productivity which are the normal sources of profit. Socialist governments of democracies should therefore be more anti-inflationary than any others, for they have always morally condemned both the private profit motive and all windfall profits to which the work of the recipients has contributed nothing: *e.g.* profits on buying and selling investments, profits on the rise in land or other real estate values due to the economic development of the community, etc.

But alas for principles in political practice! Socialist governments of democracies—for instance, in Britain, Sweden and Norway—have deliberately inflated as fast and far as any other; and while they have attempted to tax away windfall profits, they have not dared to tax them *all* away, lest the real capital equipment of the profiting concerns be rapidly eaten up by the inflation, and business failures and unemployment on a grand scale supervene. Even in inflation, therefore, Socialism has shown that ambivalent class-conscious attitude—confusing to friend and foe alike—which is best exemplified in Britain by its doctrinal opposition to the windfall profits of investors or business men alongside its political condonation of windfall profits for winners of football pools (in which the big winnings are in fact the small people's contributions). The flux of inflationary profits is therefore only an economic aspect of the social flux in all values and principles caused by inflation.

There are two other main criticisms of inflation's effects in the economic sphere. First, inflation interferes with people's normal calculations about present *versus* future values, about spending or saving, and about one kind of investment or another. By making the money measure itself alter all the time, it distorts the normally dependable structure on which businesses and individuals must found calculations of the comparative worthwhileness to themselves of possible economic actions. To offset inflation, to cope with it as an added factor in economic calculations which are complex enough without it, they must engage in economic courses which they would not follow if money were reliable, stable and sound.[1]

Secondly, businesses *must* make more profits in an inflation, in order to be able to replace their old capital equipment, when it is scrapped, with new and better kinds, but at much higher prices. The higher replacement costs must be covered by savings—either those of the business itself ('self-financing' by 'ploughed-back' profits) or those of individuals or institutions (*e.g.* insurance companies) making fresh savings and investments. In either case, governments *must* permit such savings in an inflation; else society's productive capital would run down, dragging employment and standards of life with it. So democratic governments get themselves into worse dilemmas the more they inflate. If they tax away more and more 'windfall' profits they themselves must

[1] See Chapter 4, p. 61.

steer them back into productive investment (which makes the society more and more Socialist, State-run, and totalitarian). Or they must leave those profits to the decisions of individuals, in which case—as inflation goes on—greater paper profitability will occur in businesses and undertakings which may increasingly retain those profits under their own control. New savings will thus only become available to existing concerns.

The 'hecticness' above mentioned, the distortions of values due to inflation, will thus import into all business decisions the overriding decision to defeat inflation itself. Hence disruptions of business decisions are added to the distortions of consumers' demands, as the distribution of more and more depreciating money throughout the society is itself distorted.[1]

Inflation against Growth

Of all inflationary distortions the subtlest, and possibly in the long run the most dangerous to the society, is that which disrupts the appropriate, normal, 'indicated' and requisite pattern of development and growth. The capital structure of a society at any given moment 'indicates'—implies in its very proportions—a logical, requisite pattern of further investment for both its maintenance (replacement of outworn assets or wear-and-tear) and development (extensions and expansions). This pattern is a kind of schedule through time-to-come: buildings and long-enduring assets falling due for replacement only slowly and therefore in small annual portions; 'younger' assets, like machines, falling due in greater yearly bulk; and special machines, or other capital assets for one short purpose, even falling due in two years or even less (50 per cent p.a. depreciation rate and even higher).

Inflation subtly saps this structure. It undermines confidence in savings and investment and in the future value of money. But it undermines it much more for long-term investment, less so for that at short term. Consequently the regular pattern, the logical schedule, of requisite investment ceases to be practicable. The schedule or pattern becomes heavily tilted towards short-term investments and more quickly turned-over profits in depreciating money. Longer-term assets suffer. Accordingly the entire economy gets disrupted in its production, distribution, consumption, and investment. And accordingly also the rates of development or

[1] See Chapter 4, p. 62.

growth of the economy in its component sectors—agriculture, industries, services, houses and other buildings, communications —go all awry, tilted towards the present and away from a remote future, or else tilted towards investment in assets peculiarly capable of benefiting from inflation, or capable of being quickly converted from one temporarily profitable use to another. Since inflation confers extraordinary 'windfall profits' on such shorter-term, quickly transferable, smartly 'in and out' uses of capital, it necessarily militates against a stable, steady, compounded rate of economic growth.

Yet a democratic society stands eminently in need of just such stability in its economic development in order to conserve its citizens' freedoms. A totalitarian one 'enjoys' (if that is the right word) a built-in instability of development anyway, matching its enforced rigidities, strains and stresses, and its sudden arbitrary alterations, 'according to plan'. Thus inflation as the policy of a democracy destroys the foundations for its own dependable economic growth.

No Two Kinds of Inflation

For a time there was a fashion to talk of two kinds of inflation: one due to sheer superfluity of money and credit put out by the authorities; the other termed a 'cost-push' inflation, due to up-ward pressures on money incomes from vested interests and groups whereof trades unions were chief. But it is a distinction without a difference. If the money and credit were not con-tinuously available, if employers knew that they could not pass on rising costs ('cost-push') to consumers who could pay more, no amount of 'cost-push' from trades unions or other suppliers would gain such pushers any greater money incomes. All that would happen would then be the bankrupting, or other retirement from production, of the marginal employers in line after line of acti-vity, with consequent unemployment of resources. Marginal con-sumers—unable and unwilling to pay higher prices—would leave some supplies unbought. Continuous inflation as a policy provides both producers and consumers with the extra wherewithal to pay an additional round of higher prices. Once that stops, the last round fails to sell goods and a limit is automatically put on further rises in costs, prices and money incomes.

A doctrinal dispute has arisen over this. Some political

economists say that a society will not grow at any reasonable rate without 'only a little' inflation. They point to what they call the stagnation between the world wars—omitting to notice the vast technical and other changes (*e.g.* in shipping, transport, housing) carried out in that period in America, Britain, Germany, etc. On the other hand some political economists take an extreme anti-State position, denying the State any use or duties or powers, and demanding a rigidly automatic monetary and economic system of *laissez faire*. Under such a system a world-trading society might through no fault of its own be subjected to fierce economic on-slaughts and unemployment by the actions of other nations, and be denied the right to cushion or counter them. Moreover only the State can establish and supervise the legal and other conditions to make freedom of enterprise and competition effective.

Truth, as nearly always, lies in the middle between extremes. The modern democratic State has a duty to secure not the most rapid growth, but the most rapid *reasonable* rate of growth. It must be reasonable in relation to preservation of individual and corporate freedoms, to social and political stability, to availability of enough resources 'in reserve' to meet new situations and techniques and demands, and to the stability of all money values, costs and prices upon which calculations for the future must be made. Continuous inflation, carried as a policy beyond that point, will make hay alike of democratic society and growth itself. The State will then have to round on the trades unions and other pressure-groups, instituting a compulsory 'national wage policy', freezing people in jobs and lines of business, and generally undoing the democratic system of free worker's association, free consumer's choice, and free producer's enterprise. A democratic system can only function freely and for the good of all between the extremes of outright Statism on the one hand and outright *laissez faire* on the other. Under either extreme system, democracy and personal freedoms, the social responsibility of the strong to the weak, and the cohesion of modern society alike become impossible.

It is the task of democratic government therefore to avoid the inflationary extreme on the one hand (with its trend to totalitarianism) and on the other the anarchy of extreme *laissez faire*. That means reliance on up-to-date economic information, on expert analysis, and on courageous judgments and actions for the general good and against the partial vested interests and pressure groups. These latter must squeal, as new techniques and unfore-seen developments pinch them. But if a coherent, progressive, democratic society is to persist, they must never be allowed to get what they squeal for. The purchasing power of that society's money—the measure of all material values and their inter-relationships by which alone growth itself is measurable—must be kept as stable, reliable and calculable as possible, no matter who squeals or for what.

There are other ways of cushioning and relieving the pinches of circumstance than by an indiscriminate, continuous inflation which confuses everyone and everything in a combined wage-push and cost-pull on all prices. Democracy's money should be as 'neutral' as possible. It cannot in the modern world be entirely neutral, *i.e.* utterly unmanaged and automatic like gold coinage before banknotes and credit were developed. But democracy's money should not be allowed to exert a persistently inflationary influence on prices *merely because inflation is official policy, i.e. an independently operating monetary factor in its own right.* Governments should strive to keep money to its normal role of a neutral measure—varying its supply only to preserve stability of prices and thus conserve its reliability as a measure. If they do this, we shall more accurately be able to gauge the pure effects of technical and other developments in an economic system, with-out any confusion due to monetary changes. And that will en-able us to cope with them *apart from inflationary or deflationary influences.*

Anatomy of Inflation

The confusion between so-called 'monetary' inflation and 'cost-push' (or 'wage-push') inflation arises for understandable reasons. As we have seen, any inflation in any period must result from *the rate of flow of money incomes* increasing more than *the rate of flow of goods and services on which those incomes can be spent* (including in 'goods and services' and 'spent' the investment of savings in capital equipment). Thus, there is always a race going on between the two rates of flow in any country; and to bring them into balance, so that costs and prices become stable, is al-ways a delicate and difficult task.

Technical progress, new equipment, and better methods of work are always pushing up the productive efficiency (or productivity) of all ingredients of production—more, naturally, in manufacturing, less in administrative, clerical, professional, and other 'service' occupations. So the year-to-year rise of productivity turns out more goods and services from much the same labour force, as the machinery and fuel and horse-power per worker (capital per worker) increases. This productivity rate therefore always offsets any inflation of money incomes. It varies from one country to another as capital per worker, technical know-how, and other conditions vary from country to country. In the United States, Britain, Sweden and Switzerland—countries relatively unscathed in the last war—the year-to-year rise in productivity per worker between 1950 and 1960 varied only between $1\frac{1}{2}$ and $2\frac{1}{2}$ per cent a year. In Germany, France, Japan and Russia on the other hand—countries in which conditions, for many reasons, were far different—it varied between 3 and 7 per cent a year. That is the anti-inflationary rate of flow of production.

The second inflationary rate of flow, that of money incomes, is determined at two sources. The first source is the State's and Government's own spending, its tax-revenues, levies, charges and borrowings; for all State spending goes out to become somebody's income. The second source is the arrangements of incomes between private employers and employed, the self-employed, retired, etc. This is where the confusion between 'monetary' inflation and 'cost-push' or 'wage-push' inflation begins. People get into the habit of looking *only* at one source—that of the State's monetary activities—and calling any 'deficit financing' at that source 'monetary inflation'. Or they look *only* at the other source —commonly called the industrial front, but better called the private sector—and call any agreed pushing-up of profits and other earnings a 'cost-push or 'wage-push' inflation. Yet whether there is in fact *any* inflation going on at all depends on the result of three varying factors: first, the rate of flow of goods and services available to savers-investors and purchasers, dependent among other things on the rate of technical progress (increasing productivity); secondly, the effect on balance of all the State's activities in taxing, charging, subsidising, spending, and saving-investing; and third, and only lastly, what employers and employed can do in the private sector of the economy *after* their private stage has been set for them by the State and the other monetary and credit authorities (*e.g.* the banking system, hire-purchase firms, etc).

How Inflation Arises

Whether inflation will occur—whether the general price level will rise in any period—depends on the interaction of those varying factors. For example, prices need not rise at all, though the State spends more and wages and profits and all other incomes rise (say) by 2½ per cent in any year, if only over-all productivity also rises by 2½ per cent or more. The rate of flow of goods and services, on which the extra 2½ per cent of money incomes is spent, will also have increased to match the extra money incomes. Similarly prices need not rise though the State undertakes a lot more public works of a capital kind (*e.g.* highways, railways, housing, schools, hospitals, harbours) provided it can finance them by borrowing its citizens' willing and voluntary savings to that amount—or by forcing them to save it (as in Russia) or by extra taxation of its citizens to that amount (which is forced saving)—or provided that private enterprise reduces its own investment programme by the amount the State needs, and the existing savings then get switched from private enterprise to the State.

Inflation arises in any period when the total of money incomes is allowed, or made, to rise faster than the community is prepared, or allowed, to turn out all kinds of goods and services on which the money is spent. Accordingly it can be brought about by the State and other monetary and credit authorities alone, if they merely expand the flow of money beyond the flow of goods and services. It can be brought about by both the State and private employers and employed, if the State piles over-ambitious spending programmes on top of private enterprise's own programmes, and then finances the State's programmes not by borrowing real savings but by short-term borrowings (IOU's) or other 'deficit finance'. It will always be brought about if the total of investment in any period—the total of both State and private capital programmes—amounts to more than the savings (personal, by businesses, and 'forced' from taxpayers) available, and the gap is then covered by expanding credit.

Ultimately, therefore, the control of inflation involves trimming this total of capital programmes—*i.e.* investment of all kinds, State and private—to available savings of all kinds, whether voluntary or forced by the State (in Budget surpluses of tax-revenue). But citizens demand that the State and private enterprise should simultaneously push forward with ambitious modernization and other capital programmes. They also demand continuation of 'full employment' policies, development of under-developed countries overseas by new loans, rising wages and other incomes and thus their own consumption standards at home, more State welfare services, etc, etc. If the State is administered by timid or lazy governments, inflation seems the easiest way of meeting most people's—at any rate, most productive people's—requirements in the short run.

If such governments keep the flow of money and credit *ahead of* the flow of goods and services (productivity), the State's own clients and beneficiaries will get what they want (in money); employers will all make enough (paper) profits to cover rising wage and other costs and yet survive; trade unions will all get from employers what they push for (in money); and for that short run only the non-productive pensioners, retired folk, and other receivers of fixed money incomes will suffer from the inevitably rising prices.

But short runs become long. The longer inflation of this kind goes on, the more prices rise. The greater, then, become the inflationary problems; for it becomes increasingly difficult to control inflation. For example, individuals and businesses stick to their savings and profits or invest them only in their own concerns or in ordinary shares in private business, and refuse to lend to the State at long or medium term. That forces the State in turn to rely more and more on short-term finance for its programmes, which in turn increases the inflationary potential (the basis for the banking system's supply of credit). Again, trade unions and employers start to discount the rate of inflation—the rate of rise in prices—in their wage-demands and profits; which pushes costs and prices higher, and so outpaces faster than ever the rise in productivity. (While productivity rose at roughly the same rate in the USA and Britain between 1950 and 1960, the greater British inflation in that period pushed British prices up at 50 per cent more than the American rate of price-rise.) Technical progress and productivity do not stand a chance of yielding their best fruits once inflation has been allowed to become a built-in, long-run affair. They only stand their chance of doing so—of thus helping to maintain sound money and true costs and other values—if the Government, the State, and the monetary and credit authorities first give them elbow-room in which to operate. That room can only be provided by sound currency itself, on which all calculations can be based. And that can only be provided by abjuring inflation as a policy.

Controls Over Credit

Among governments' instruments for producing or reducing inflation are what economists call 'open market operations'. Briefly these are purchases or sales of government 'gilt-edged' bonds or other longer-term IOU's in the market by a government's agents. Thus if the government's agents bid at prices attractive enough—*i.e.* at higher than market prices—they will get such bonds by pushing up their prices, and thus pushing down the annual yield of interest on them, which is pushing down the long-term interest rate. They will then be paying cash out to these bonds' former owners. The new cash will come from the government, who in turn secure it by issuing new short-term IOUs (bills) to the government's bankers, who in their turn create new credit against them for the government to draw on: *i.e.* new overdrafts, if you like. This process simply converts what was a long-term locked-up saving—a medium- or long-term government bond—into liquid cash. It increases liquidity. It lowers interest rates. It stimulates enterprisers to borrow, since the owner of the new cash must do something with it. If he merely buys another security, he merely passes on his cash to the seller who inherits the headache 'what to do with the cash?' At some point, with someone, the extra liquidity will be put to work: buying some goods and services, whether consumer's or producer's (capital) goods, and thus employing more resources—or calling more forth—than were till then employed.

That is an example of an 'open market operation' designed to expand a country's purchasing-power and economic activity. It is useful in a recession or depression when unemployed resources lie idle and available. *Per contra* it is the worst possible proceeding, a flagrant abuse and an aggravation of inflation, whenever resources are already fully or over-fully employed: overstoking the boiler.

But there is nothing wrong with the mechanism in itself. It works both ways. It is a most useful counter to inflation. The government's agents can equally go into the open market and mop up businesses' and people's too-great liquid cash and other short-term liquid assets, by selling to them new medium- or long-term IOUs (bonds). They will only be able to sell such new 'gilt-edged' to them at attractive prices: *i.e.* since it is an inflationary situation they will have to offer the new bonds, locking up people's money for some years to come, at a higher interest rate, a higher yield, than has hitherto ruled in the market. So to counter inflation by this means the government will raise the long-term interest rate. It will be converting what were liquid assets (cash, 'shorts', bank deposits) into investments in bonds for a longish period to come. On balance it will be locking up immediate purchasing-power, mopping it up into the authorities' hands, *but not to be spent again by the government* either on its current or its capital account. Instead the mopped-up purchasing-power will be used to cancel some of the government's short-term or floating debt, its bills in the banking system. When these bills run out at due dates, the government will simply pay them off; fewer will lie in the banks' portfolios; and so the banks' power to expand credit on them as a basis will be cut down, together with the government's own deposits at the banks. Liquidity will diminish. Credit will tighten or be 'squeezed'.

This anti-inflationary or dis-inflationary action is termed 'funding' government indebtedness, because it converts liquid assets into 'funded debt' (long-term bonds). To be really effective, it must turn such liquid assets into il-liquid (long-term) assets on balance: *i.e.* over and above the government's needs to spend on both current and capital accounts, it must mop up some liquid assets and 'fund' them. In other words, over and above the government's receipts from tax-revenues, ordinary savings, and ordinary government borrowings at both short and long term, the government must also mop up some purchasing-power by these 'open market operations' and convert it into long-term investment. It must switch some people or businesses or institutions holding short-term government IOUs (bills) out of them, and into long—or at any rate longer—term bonds. It must reduce floating, but expand funded, government debt. In that way it will curtail the total of credit in the country, by curtailing its own bills (short-term debt) at the banks. As bank deposits form the bulk of all money in a modern industrial society, this curtailing of the banks' ability to create fresh credit on balance will very quickly have its restraining effect upon purchasing-power, and thus upon inflation.

Of course buyers of the government's new long-term bonds can at once sell them again for cash; but in that case they merely do, in the opposite direction, what we saw the sellers of bonds to the government's agents doing above: they will merely be passing on the headache to others. The cash has got to come from somebody or some institution in the long line of transactions; and in the end it is frozen into long-term bonds, in exchange for a government promise to pay interest on it and to repay the principal some years later.

Naturally there are many refinements of detail in these 'open market operations' into which it is not necessary to enter here. Suffice it to say that both the inflationary and deflationary uses of them—or, to use current cant, the reflationary (expansionist) and disinflationary (contractionist) uses of them—are indicated as required in any industrially developed democracy from time to time, as its economic resources are either under-employed (when more immediate purchasing-power is indicated) or overstrained (when less purchasing-power is required). The control of such monetary operations lies, like that over money itself, in the hands of governments. They alone have the powers to tax, the powers to create or cancel government debt, and the powers therefore to swell or restrain the flow of purchasing-power. If governments manage a country's finances—which are their own finances—aright, they can secure sound money, a reasonably stable price level, and therefore steady economic growth. There is nothing in the financial mechanisms of modern democracies making inflation inevitable or uncontrollable. Its causes lie in politics, not economics. If governments cannot withstand vested interests pressing for more government spending, they cannot reduce taxes, or reduce government borrowing, and counter inflation. Thus behind the economics of inflation lies its politics.

PART III

WHY?

CHAPTER 6

DEMOCRATIC MYTHS AND METHODS

Democracy, representative government, and universal adult suffrage go difficultly with modern technical society. The new techniques form vested interests of their own. They render older vested interests, clustered around older methods, fearfully rigid and anxiously tenacious. The specialization and sub-specialization of all kinds of human work, the mechanization of so much of everyday life, the growing bigness of business and civil administration, the expansion of the State's duties and powers over more and more details of its citizens' daily lives—these increasingly make modern societies depend on smooth co-ordination and articulated functioning. They make them complex, sensitive, vulnerable. If the co-ordination and articulation are interrupted, thrown out of mesh, a whole society now breaks down, whereas less than 200 years ago the effects of political, military and economic disruptions were confined to the space of a day's ride on horseback.

The government of a modern industrial democracy finds itself the focus of contending vested interests. Its farmers are organized to extract from the State, by taxes or subsidies or artificial high prices for their produce, a levy upon the technical advances of industry—which prevents under-developed countries overseas from selling more of their produce to the industrial democracy and buying the products of its industrial population in return. Its industrialists clamour for protection from foreign competition, and for relief from the high taxes necessitated by the State's welfare schemes. Its trade unions, developed in days of poverty and oppression, now as much opposed to each other's 'differentials' as to employers, act as pressure-groups on the State agencies and private employers to secure monopoly profits for their members. These latter and their families are now on balance the beneficiaries of all the new or expanded State welfare, at the cost of all taxpayers (including themselves). So the demands on the public purse of the modern industrial democracy become crushing.

To fulfil them, the State raises taxes upon private enterprises and the more productive or more responsible individuals to penal heights where they become disincentives to enterprise, creative initiative and responsibility. When taxes on individual and corporate persons become intolerably high, the State has recourse to inflation to pay its own bills for its ever-mounting expenditure, to keep 'full employment' going, and to pay all the subsidies and other demands of vested interests. Once inflation is pursued as a fund-raising policy, it is to the advantage of all to be debtors rather than creditors, to pay even a high rate of interest on loans rather than to receive it (since it is a cost or expense allowed against taxes), to spend rather than save, and to 'bump up' all costs and expenses. And at that point the feet of a democratic society are already well advanced along the primrose way.

Clearly the obvious way to avoid inflation, then, is for the State, the government, not to give in to the demands of the voters arrayed in their various vested interests and pressure-groups; not to keep up steam for 'full employment' of all resources, so that group interests become vested and their demands irresistible. But that is precisely what the leading democracies did not do after 1945. They gave in to any and every vested interest, and created new ones by inflation. The great post-war inflation coincided with 'full employment' as a policy. But 'full employment' almost everywhere was interpreted as the employment of everyone who wanted to work, and at any job old or new, without distinctions about efficiency or economy or comparative costs. Inflation alone, persistently cumulative, could realize such a definition. It was justified in the name of Lord Keynes who, before the war, had done much—and justifiably—to popularize the need to employ to reasonable fullness a nation's resources so that none lay idle and wasted.

Keynes Misappropriated

Keynes talked of a continuous fall in interest rates until 'the euthanasia of the *rentier*' came about, and even of a negative rate of interest (when savers would pay fines to save). He talked and wrote during the bad old days of idle and wasted resources, wanting to employ them productively. But he carefully emphasized the dangers of inflation: of carrying 'managed money' so far and so persistently that 'full employment' of all resources became 'over-full', shortages developed all round, queues formed, the currency went rapidly to pot, and society disintegrated. None was more insistent than he on every government's need to manage money so that saving and investment continued to be worthwhile, prices were kept comparatively stable, the progress of productivity showed itself more by *reducing* costs and prices, and taxes were raised and budget surpluses created in times of boom (and taxes reduced and budget deficits created whenever recessions began). His advocacy of 'managed money' was never an undiscriminating recommendation of constant, continuous, cumulative inflation halving any currency's purchasing power in a decade.

Those who, since his death in 1946, have pled him in aid to justify such inflationary excesses have had their eyes mainly on social and political revolutions to be achieved by monetary means. That was something Keynes condemned more sharply than anything else. He had more in common with Lord Beveridge and the latter's statistical advisers (most of them Socialists) who, preparing *Full Employment in a Free Society*[1] in the war, advocated an *average* long-term figure of 3 per cent of unemployed persons at any time; whereas the *average* in Britain from 1950 to 1960 was below 1½ per cent, less than half the Beveridge recommendation. Keynes could hardly have disagreed with the Beveridge figure, for his humane and fertile mind had seized at the very outbreak of war the social dangers of a 'siege-inflation'. Accordingly he at once published *How to Pay For the War*[2], a plan to mop up and immobilize the proportion of people's purchasing power which—'for the duration'— could not be spent on normal peacetime goods and services no longer available. He was thereby the 'onlie begetter' of the unpopular British 'post-war credits': an extra wartime income-tax intended to stand to people's credit until redeemable in peacetime when normal production supplied once more the necessary consumers' goods and services.[3] The

[1] Allen & Unwin, 1944.
[2] Macmillan, 1940.
[3] See also Chapter 2, p. 27.

scheme was sound: as sound as his earlier programme for managing money so that booms were damped down by it and recessions filled in.

What went wrong was not Keynes's schemes. It was his optimism about politics, politicians, employers and trades unionists. They ensured after the war, in combination against timid governments, that money was only managed to secure perpetual inflation, to achieve continuous boom conditions. Consequently the wartime 'siege-inflation' went on: the post-war credits could not be repaid. When the inevitable punctuating crises occurred—as they regularly did for example, in France, Britain, Holland, Sweden, etc—money was not managed to compensate the booms, halt inflation, and keep prices and moneys stable. Devaluations of currencies were preferred, physical controls on all kinds of economic activity were applied in panic, and after far-going economic convulsions the inflationary process was resumed. Keynes would have been the foremost to denounce such behaviour as the doom of democracy.

Inflation Not Vital to Growth

Yet the British Labour Party and its chief financial supporters, the trade unions, when in power from 1945 to 1951, pursued a steady 3 to 5 per cent inflation as a matter of policy. Simultaneously they put penal taxation on individuals and businesses, but demanded more saving and investment by companies and individuals, and more foreign lending by Britain. They still demand these things in the 1960s. The irreconcilability of such policies— which enormously encourage consumption and penalize saving —is scarcely perceived. Inflation in the last fifteen years has heavily advantaged the Labour Party's supporters—who are most of the beneficiaries of the Welfare State and most of the trades unions' members. They have now emerged with a net advance of 30 per cent in real income per head since 1938 on average. But the net advantage to this newly-privileged class was not wholly—not even mainly—derived from the rise in output per head, i.e. from productivity. It was mainly derived from redistribution of the comparatively lagging national income between the penalized groups in favour of the others, by way of taxation (positive Government policy) and inflation (negative Government policy).[1]

[1] See Chapter 3, p. 49.

On the other hand the inflation allowed lazy and unenterprising employers to settle for an easy, cosy, salaried life, with adequate inflationary *paper* profits; but in reality they were eating their seed corn, consuming their original capital. A premium was thus put on waste, inefficiency and consumption.

Continuous inflation is not needed to ensure the fullest economical use of a nation's resources and the most rapid rate of growth. At least Russia's progress—albeit under a dictatorship—shows that. But so does the progress in standards of living, with relatively more stable price-levels and no periodic crises or devaluations, of Americans, Swiss, Germans and Japanese after the war. They are democracies, too. They have strong—some of them, *e.g.* the United States, have militant—trade unions. And they have had employment percentages as stable as those of the inflating democracies like Sweden, Britain and France. Inflation is an ever-present danger, even among them and even today; but that is no detraction from their long success in averting or restraining it.

What is Democracy?

Democracy is not always good or safe; it is assuredly not always right; and it does not always guarantee to its citizens, individually or in their associations, their basic freedoms of action and expression. The democratic process of creating a 'mixed economy' brings with it great dangers for the individual citizen. Accordingly that process deserves to be better understood by the citizenry.

It is entirely democratic for a majority of the electorate, in a country run by universal adult suffrage and representative government, to pass laws altering the value of money and contracts, preventing anyone engaging in trade, taking away people's property, compelling all children to receive the same State education in the same subjects, making adultery a crime, stopping citizens travelling abroad or foreigners coming in, decreeing all production and all consumption, and freezing everyone in their occupations. Only in democracies enjoying the safeguards of a written constitution guaranteeing personal liberties, and where some other body than the government of the day has powers to enforce them, can universal suffrage and representative government be safe from 'the worst tyranny of all' (in the words of De Tocqueville, John Stuart Mill, Walter Bagehot, James F. Stephen,

Lord Acton and many another): that of the majority over the minority. Generally only federal states and constitutions are so governed.

Without such safeguards, democracy and representative government can easily slip into the hands of one party in a temporary majority. That one party can forthwith abolish basic liberties, undo society, refashion it overnight in that one party's image, and deny to all minorities their own ways of life in favour of the supporters of the majority party alone. All of this would be 'democratic' in the literal sense of that much-used, much-abused term. All of it would equally be 'representative'. All of it might be egalitarian. But it would be neither just nor equitable; for it is unjust and inequitable to treat equals in certain things unequally, or unequals in certain things equally. Thus a personal dictator, despot or tyrant might be more just and equitable to *all* his subjects than a tyrannous, despotic, dictatorial democracy, run by a man or an oligarchy duly elected by a majority of the citizens in the name, and by the method, of representative government.

Democracy and the State

This is no treatise on political philosophy, theory, or practice. But it is necessary these days to clear much public misunderstanding from the terms of democracy. The vestigial democracies of the free half of the world—certainly those which are already industrialized—have made themselves 'mixed economies' by undertaking in the sphere of their citizens' economic affairs, by and with the powers of the State (*i.e.* of the temporary majority as a Government), responsibilities and functions formerly fulfilled by citizens in free competition. Most of the State's 'mixture' in these remaining democracies has occurred this century. Most of it has been in the spheres of monetary control, economic relations with other countries, defence, communications, fuel and power, and of the minimal standards of hygiene, health and material welfare for their citizens. Most of it has come about 'democratically'; that is, a majority has voted for each advance of the State into the economic sphere, or has at least ratified it after the event, no matter which political party formed the temporary government.

This has gone on in America as well as in Western European democracies (where it began). And now, on the plea that an 'affluent society' needs more Federal Government taxing and spending to lay down 'appropriate' goals of production and consumption, and keep up a desirable rate of growth, American voices are raised to demand more and more State activities and powers in the economic field. The economy of the American democracy—and, since it leads the world in output per head, presumably therefore of all others—'should', according to this argument, become more and more 'mixed'.

By its very nature—arrogance towards freedom of consumers' and producers' choices, collective *dirigisme*, and economic determinism by a knowing *élite* or minority of controllers—this argument arouses suspicion. Whither does it lead? Where is it to stop? Why 'should' it stop anywhere short of complete 100 per cent totalitarianism? In that case what can logically distinguish it from Communism, Socialism, or other eventually authoritarian social systems?

Too much State activity, too rapidly, means too much State spending. Too much State spending too fast means a rapid multiplication of State controls to stop private spending: that is, restrictions on production and consumption *plus* higher taxes. Rapidly rising, or too high, taxes on individuals and companies mean a building-up of costs, since persons and firms take account of the high or rising taxes in their prices. Plumbers, actors, lawyers, trade unionists, farmers, businessmen, all ask for their remuneration at levels which will allow them to live as they feel they and their families should live net of taxes; *i.e.* they seek for fees, wages, profits that give them a net purchasing power at *their own* command, after the State has taken its various 'cuts' or taxes.

This has been seen at its worst since 1945 in the British and Swedish democracies, where inflation has concomitantly shown itself acutely, where the currency has accordingly badly depreciated, but where the citizens and companies have loyally (and more honourably than elsewhere) paid their penally high taxes. In some other remaining democracies they have contrived not to, and inflation has consequently been even more acute. But that does not detract from the principle: namely, that if the majority's demand on a democracy is for more and more State activity, responsibility, and power in its economy, the majority's demand is really one for higher taxes, more State controls, and less economic freedom for *all* citizens. As this soon becomes apparent to a democracy's Parliament, press, and public, the government tries to avoid the necessary unpopularity of taxing and controlling people more.

Published, known, formal, recognized taxes are pushed to their upper limit: a limit of toleration for persons and companies alike. Those limits involve controls enough, in all conscience: for instance, penalties for trying to get property out of the democratic country's jurisdiction, inability to travel abroad, even inability (as in Britain until the 1950s) to change certain businesses from making one thing to making another. To this day the top rates of tax on individuals' incomes in Britain, Norway and Sweden are the highest in the world. They act as penalties on success. One year's gross earnings out of every four are taken by the State from top executives, skilled managers, and leaders of the State's own public services. Such State penalization of administrative responsibility, productive skill, and creative enterprise, quickly broadens down, at lower but still heavily penalized levels of income, to racketeering, 'fiddling', black marketing, and other illicit dealing. These are already familiar ways of evading fiscal laws which have strained and snapped traditional morality. By being suddenly made too onerous for ordinary mortals, democracy's fiscal demands bring all law and order into contempt.

When such a stage is reached in the democratic process of rapidly creating a 'mixed economy' (by greatly expanding State economic activities at the cost of private economic enterprise) inflation as a deliberate instrument and policy of government is inevitable. It has in all probability been going on, secretly and subtly, for some time already, and has therefore been playing its historic rôle of helping to bring such a state of affairs in a society about. From that point or stage there are only two roads: one leading on to the overthrow of democracy and personal freedoms altogether; the other leading back to sound money and a reasonable balance between State and private economic action, upon which personal freedoms depend.

Myths of Democracy

Much public sufferance of inflation in modern democracies is due to party politics, particularly (but by no means entirely) to Communist, Socialist and other collectivist ideologies. The modern mass-voters in an industrial democracy are also mass-producers and mass-consumers. They have been led by political and economic organizations to believe in party-political mass-myths, which are important working-parts of a mass-ideology: *e.g.* that wages rising faster than productivity need not be inflationary; that only 'the rich' need be despoiled by inflation and progressive taxation; that trade unions can always get 'one jump ahead' of inflation, by putting upon 'the rich' the real cost of all wage increases larger than the rise in productivity; that companies can be forced to reduce profits and dividends permanently in favour of wages; that perpetual inflation offers all other sections of society no defences, but only a defence to trade unions; and so on.

One such myth is that 'full employment' (meaning no temporary unemployment) and the most rapid economic growth can only come by a steady and persistent inflation. It is a myth because it is an element of faith or belief, irrational and not proven. Indeed, the opposite proposition—that reasonably full employment and more rapid economic growth in the masses' material welfare (including leisure) could come by avoiding inflation and by the consequently greater adaptability—is more rationally probable. This is because the discoveries and applications of science, and the consequent sudden needs to modify and adapt and render flexible a modern economy, are unpredictable and unplannable.

In the mythology of the Left in the remaining West European democracies (not in the United States, where there is no Left at all in the original European sense) inflation as a policy is treated as a way of expropriating 'the capitalists', as well as a way of securing perpetual 'full employment' and economic growth by forced savings. Higher taxation of these same capitalists (mainly companies) is then made to yield—among other things—enough to recompense pensioners and other 'reputable' receivers of fixed money incomes (*e.g.* small savers) for the inevitable loss of their purchasing power year by year. Left-wing Governments thus push taxation of higher incomes (individuals' and businesses') to penally high levels, but defray their rising running and other current costs, all of which they are naturally boosting at the same time, by the deliberate inflation.

The 'forced savings' by the State thus generally and largely fail in a democracy to become 'forced investments'. They go mainly on current consumption, either in welfare and subsidies to lower income brackets or in additions to the pensioners' or small savers' incomes by the 'beneficent' governments to correspond with their depreciation of the currency. In that way the minority of productive, responsible, enterprising or highly skilled persons—the main source of initiative and personal savings—is penalized by 'progressive' taxation in favour of the great majority of current consumers, a number of whom are not productive.

Irrationality and mythology become apparent in all this as soon as one delves into the evidence. One discovers that a policy of perpetual inflation certainly secures 'full employment', but only by making work—not what work turns out, or at what cost, or for whom—the main criterion of growth; that if expropriation of capitalists occurs merely to defray *current* spending, forced savings from the entire community become imperative for *capital* investment, and then the government has to raise them, not from the expropriated minority but from the masses themselves (as in Russia); that individual freedoms progressively disappear; and that such a society cannot long remain a democracy. It will last as a democracy an even shorter time, the more dependent its people are for their material welfare on competitive foreign trade.

That was what Lord Keynes meant when he declared that debauching a currency sapped the foundations of a society more subtly, swiftly and permanently than any other conspiracy. The society which emerges after a period under such a policy of inflation is different. More important, it has to be run differently. So a democratic government may embark on such a policy; but it can only pursue it by controlling and repressing more and more; and it quickly becomes non-democratic. That may be all right as long as it is what such parties and governments want. But if they really do not want it, it is as shortsighted and stupid as policies making compulsory the use of out-of-date fuels, materials, machines, industries or methods. These only tax the community, and hold up technical progress and economic growth, on behalf of a small minority's vested interest: like refusing to allow a new machine to cut unit-costs and spread products more widely by turning out all of which it is capable. Far from being social dynamics and progress, it is social statics and retrogression.

Democracy and Totalitarianism

'The preponderance of mythical thought over rational thought in some of our modern political systems is obvious.'[1] Our wonderful modern communications—a cheap and excellent press, television, radio, high personal mobilities by private and public vehicles, longer leisure with more travel—make the spread of such irrational myths, slogans, and other political party dogmas easier than the spread of logic and reason. Their emotional appeal is naturally to the overwhelming majority in a mass electorate; for that less-inquiring majority is naturally the least rational and least aware of the evidence for rational conclusions.

Later in this book[2] we confront 'the American way' with that of the Russians. It is worth emphasizing here how far back the causes of such a contemporary confrontation go. They go back through two markedly opposed streams of opinion about politics and society.

'The American way' still reposes more than any other (save that of the Swiss) on individual freedoms: on man as an end in himself, striving with freedom of choice to realize more and more of his potentialities in self-expression, and by his own (and others') trial and error utilizing all freedoms of self-expression. It goes back along a path of rational philosophy to Kant, the apostle of eighteenth-century Enlightenment and reason, of personal freedoms, and of man as an end who must never be used by other men as a means.

The way of the Russians and other totalitarians also goes back to the eighteenth century, but along the pathway of myth, unreason, and determinism. Along that path we find people like Hitler, Spengler, Nietzsche, Marx, Gobineau and Hegel. (They by no means agreed with each other.) Hegel's absolute State as the realization of the Fashioning Spirit on earth, supreme in might (and therefore in right) above all else on earth, is as deterministic as Marx's inevitable dictatorship of the proletariat fashioning a classless society (though Marx claimed to have 'stood Hegel on his head'). All of these irrational, fatalistic philosophers of history and society push individual freedoms into the background and proclaim the might or the freedom of the State (whatever that means) as right and pre-eminent. They look

[1] *The Myth of the State*, by E. Cassirer, OUP. 1946, p. 3.
[2] See Chapter 8, p. 123.

on individual men as means, not ends. Society is the end, not those who compose it. The State is not made for man, man is made for the State. The collective whole is greater than the sum of its parts.

But then they betray themselves. They then say that the big irrational, swarming mass—more earthy and elemental than the minority of highly developed and rational individuals—must be 'led' by its minority for a while. Only that minority—a Marx, Lenin, Stalin, the Party oligarchs, the Leader—are qualified to know and interpret what is fixed and determined for the whole Society 'far beyond the stars'. Many of them—Marx, Hitler, Stalin—did not even look 'far beyond the stars' for guidance, as did Hegel. Their own earthly might and that of their State was right, and it was quite enough for them.

It is worth remarking that the *non-collectivist* party politics of America, Britain, and other modern democracies—known as Conservative and Liberal, or Republican and Democrat—still show a few traces of ideologies from their past. But they do not now repose upon myths and doctrines. They are overwhelmingly empirical, pragmatic, practical; not 'for all time' like a faith or dogma, but serving the citizenry as best they think they can in their own times. They do not set ahead of themselves some ideal human society on earth, conceived *a priori* or 'revealed' (as in a religion) as being the best, to the realization of which by State action all individual citizens must meanwhile submit and con- form, at no matter what cost to them as individuals. British Liberalism and Toryism today, like Americans' Republican or Democrat politics, are not founded upon anything else than the best that temporary governments can do to help *all* individuals to gain more leisure and welfare for their fullest self-realiza- tion—not even, and not just, to help 'the workers' or 'the masses' but also to help the more creative and responsible minorities who are the necessary *élites* in any progressive society. These are there- fore matters of day-to-day expedients and policy, not of philosophy, ideology, dogma or myth. They admit of tentatives, reversals, trial and error, flexibility, adaptability to the unknown and unforeseeable—whereas the *a priori* ideologies of totalitarians admit only of ideological schisms, social revolutions, and crises of faith whenever something unknown and unforeseeable makes hay of their ideologies, myths, dogmas and doctrines.

The Necessity of Flexibility

The *a posteriori* nature of democratic Conservatism and Liberalism (however represented in one or another political party) gives more freedom to governments for variation and experience, for originality and initiative, for *ad hoc* learning from small-scale experiments. So, too, governments of true democracies—pledged to conserve and enlarge the scope of the individual citizens freely to choose their own means of self-realization—should not run their economic affairs by doctrines and dogmas, myths and slogans masquerading as policies, or fatalistic and deterministic secular religions decreeing this or that economic measure as inevitable.

The Open Society, the free society, does not claim to know all the social or economic answers beforehand. Not having such a secular religion and mythology, it has no way of knowing beforehand all the social and economic questions which will arise in human society as human knowledge discovers and applies more and more. So it reposes its policies on freedoms, flexibility and adaptability in order to be able the better to cope with the unforeseeable. This seems more reasonable, and rational, political behaviour than that of the so-called 'planned societies' whose governments loudly vaunt the rationality of their plans while reposing on irrational ideologies, myths, doctrines and dogmas.

'It is beyond the power of philosophy to destroy the political myths. A myth is in a sense invulnerable. It is impervious to rational arguments; it cannot be refuted by syllogisms. But philosophy can do us another important service. It can make us understand the adversary. In order to fight an enemy you must know him. That is one of the first principles of a sound strategy. To know him means not only to know his defects and weaknesses; it means to know his strength. All of us have been liable to underrate this strength. When we first heard of the political myths we found them so absurd and incongruous, so fantastic and ludicrous that we could hardly be prevailed upon to take them seriously. By now it has become clear to all of us that this was a great mistake. We should not commit the same error a second time.'[1]

Inflation conducted as a policy, or permitted by political laziness and cowardice, stems from such a political myth: the myth

[1] *Cassirer op. cit.*, p. 296.

that 'full employment' and the most rapid economic growth can best come by deliberate inflation. The first step to abandoning or avoiding it must be its proclamation, description and recognition as myth, and as a myth that grievously misleads.

Reason against Myth

One often hears the queries 'Why don't citizens of a democracy see the dangers of persistent inflation? Why don't they insist by their votes on its avoidance? Why don't higher-money-wage-demanders in their sectional organizations—why don't employees of State services—realize that the pressure of their vested interests merely pushes up the the cost of living against their own interests? Why don't people see that the prior raising of productivity—not the lagging raising of it *after* the granting of higher pay—is the cure for inflation? Why don't they all see that a diminution of the over-full employment of *all* resources, and in particular of what the State undertakes to spend *in toto*, would allow unit-costs and prices and the cost of living to come down?'

To these questions there are many valid answers. First, the popular interest in, and aptitude for, economic questions is limited; whereas the citizen's immediate interests seem to lie in his or her job and its pay, his or her labour or professional organization, his or her industry or occupational grouping. The national, communal interest takes a lowly place in popular concern, although in economic affairs what harms it harms most of the component parts of it. Secondly, according to the varying degrees of political blackmail by organized pressure-groups, the stronger of such groups do in fact manage to escape unscathed by inflation. As we saw,[1] *most weekly wage-earners in Britain contrived to push their real economic gains ahead of the rise in the cost of living*, owing to a governmental combination of persistent inflation, over-full employment, and penally progressive taxation. Once this occurs, inflation is already being discounted ahead of itself. Thirdly, public education in current affairs always lags long behind them. Despite our wonderful modern media of public communication, entertainment and diversion take precedence over information and orientation.

Fourthly, 'the masses' always believe what they most want to

[1] See Chapter 3, p. 50.

believe; and more pay in money always seems preferable, despite any subsequent rise in prices, to stable money pay accompanied by falling prices. If this human belief in gambler's luck were not so ingrained, lotteries, betting, and football pools would long since have failed to command such universal support by 'the masses'. These latter always believe, individually, they *may* be the one in a million to win. So they believe, too, that the amount of extra money pay they may win will more than recompense them for the subsequent inflation thus caused.

Fifthly, all parties of the political Left positively propagand for inflation, and urge their supporters' claims to higher money pay at the alleged cost of 'the rich'. Once full employment of all resources has been secured by the initial inflationary 'cranking-up',[1] persistent inflation does not, however, merely 'soak the rich'. It soaks the entire community, and especially those who are not organized to secure their demands for more money income. It drives up all costs and prices. Henceforth any State action to shield the defenceless sufferers from inflation drives up taxes on all the others, too. So a 'free for all' develops, unleashed not by the political Right but by the Left itself. In such a 'free for all' the supporters of the Left likely to do best out of it are the most tightly organized workers: the trades unions.

Sixth and lastly, the only cure for inflation is the prior, persistent raising of overall productive efficiency—overall productivity—at as fast a rate as, or at a rate faster than, the rise in the flow of money and credit in the society. But this is a complex concept to convey to 'the masses'. Moreover it applies in the first place to the society's output and income *as a whole*, after which the natural 'higgling of the market' settles what income each citizen can get. Very humanly and naturally, the citizen fails to spot his or her particular interest in the vast general interest; so he or she prefers to push, through some smaller organization, for what seems to be his or her immediate material interest. Thus, appeals and exhortations—so beloved of British Chancellors of the Exchequer during the fifteen post-war years—for 'restraint' in pressing for higher particular money incomes, or for reduced

---

[1] This was termed *Ankurbelung* in the democratic Germany of the 1930-33 depression before Hitler, and 'deficit finance' by Keynes and his American followers at the same date in the Anglo-Saxon world. See Chapter 2, p. 26.

prices, or for higher productivity first of all, always fall on pre-conditioned deaf ears.

These, then, are the irrational majority's answers to rational—and therefore the minority's—queries. But that does not mean the majority is right. It only means that it is human and natural. The problem for a society which hopes to remain democratic is to convince irrationality of its greater material interest in the triumph of reason : no mean undertaking.

CHAPTER 7

TRIAL BY INFLATION

It is scarcely surprising that poverty-ridden masses in countries which have recently gained sovereign independence—but little else to improve their people's welfare—should unquestioningly accept the trials of deliberate inflation, on top of the trials their ancestors suffered, in exchange for promises of economic growth and better times. But the relationship of identity drawn in industrial democracies between inflation and economic growth needs analysis. For it is a mythical relationship. It is not logically necessary. It is irrational. Yet it is certainly politically useful in industrially advanced democracies, both to lazy, shortsighted or timorous governments of the Centre and Right, and to those of the Left who are all of that and also perhaps subtly farsighted. This explains the easy acceptance of the no-growth-without-inflation myth among almost all sections of Western Europe's industrial democracies (save only the German and the Swiss).

The no-growth-without-inflation myth, so widely disseminated and accepted in all political parties and social groupings, accounts for most of the rapid rates at which, and the high peaks to which, post-war inflation was allowed to go in these West European democracies. The myth took control of all democratic party politics between 1944 and 1957-59. It even took precedence over the age-old differences between, say, Conservatives and Socialists (as in Britain). Both parties lent themselves willingly to the myth.

In those democracies at stages of decline (if not decadence) following the second exhausting World War within twenty-one years, the further social discipline and effort needed to found recovery and growth upon sound money seemed a superhuman requirement. To the Germans, who had suffered and endured even worse things and had been left with little for the second time in a generation, sound money seemed logically and imperatively the foundation for the most necessary, most rapid and most enduring economic growth. To the Swiss, who had watched belligerents and safeguarded neutrality throughout that troubled generation of wars without being directly involved in them, growth-without-inflation seemed natural. Thus all West European democracies after the war, save only Germany and Switzerland, slipped easily into inflation as a policy, no matter which party, parties or ideologies governed them.

They were rather like 'underdeveloped countries' in their mood: war-ravaged, impoverished, aware of vast needs of new capital, at their wits' end to see whence new savings might come. Though still democracies, there was tacit agreement between their nominally opposed politicians that 'forced savings' from their masses and classes alike, coupled with State controls, rationing, licences, etc, could alone bring about swift enough economic growth and recovery. None of them showed, in public opinion or political life, the bold vigour of Germany under Dr Erhard in 1948 in stablishing a new currency and keeping it as a sound foundation before all else was built upon it.

In the event, post-war growth and recovery only came to the West European democracies—Germany included—from America. The European Recovery Programme and the Organization for European Economic Co-operation were both offspring of the Marshall Plan of June 1947. They rescued European democracy. By 1949 the inevitable devaluations of the leading European democracies' currencies followed. Not even thereafter, however, was the no-growth-without-inflation myth abandoned as an all-party affair. The devaluations of 1949 placed more inflationary fuel at the disposal of the stokers. These stokers, drawn from nominally opposed political parties, fed the furnaces for a further eight years, during which the pound sterling lost a further 30 per cent of its purchasing power. Inflation was not abandoned in Britain until the courageous resignation of the Conservative Chancellor of the Exchequer, Mr Peter Thorneycroft, in 1957—over about £50m. in a Budget of over £5,000m., but on a monumental principle. For he resigned in protest against his own Prime Minister's, Cabinet's and Party's long-standing policy of national economic growth with inflation as an instrument to secure it. The last of the four major sterling crises after 1945 occurred largely as a result of his resignation. So did the new, anti-inflationary Conservative monetary policy which that fourth crisis forced his successor at the Treasury to deploy, for the first time in a dozen post-war years. The soaring of Bank Rate to 7 per cent at the end of 1957—a peak unattained for twenty-five years—marked the end of 'cheap money'. It was Thorneycroft medicine, administered by a *locum*.

It was also the beginning of the end of the no-growth-without-inflation myth. Within twelve months of the end of 1957 the Fourth Republic fell in France. By 1959 sterling and a new franc were riding 'high, wide and handsome' on an unfamiliar wave of worldwide confidence. The industrial democracies of Europe were staging a rate of economic growth-without-inflation which impressed Americans. America and Germany in their turn had become menaced by inflation, and were now the chief industrial democracies fighting the no-growth-without-inflation myth.

Political Causes and Economic Effects

This brief tour of the post-war democratic horizon raises intriguing questions. First, if the United States and Germany were able to keep out of the inflationary race from 1948 to 1958, why did they get into it in 1959 when the others got out? In the case of Germany, the answer could be 'over-full employment': by 1960 the fifteen-year-long flight of Germans from Communist East to democratic West had practically ceased; the labour market was overstrained; and trade unions were pressing hard—in a strong bargaining position for the first time—for big increases in wages. All German resources were strained at once by a boom which threatened to turn into inflation in default of appropriate restraining action by the authorities on Dr Erhard's successful lines. If this is right, inflation in an industrial democracy is ultimately due to the organized power of the workers to take more out of the National Income (a) than others can, (b) than they themselves put in, or (c) than the democracy can withstand.

But nothing of the kind was true of the American economy. There was unused industrial capacity and unemployed manpower in America. Consumption trades boomed; but capital goods trades did not. Certainly trade unions in both sectors of industry—and outside industry altogether—pressed for higher wages than the rise in productivity (either in the industries or occupations concerned or on the average in the country) justified. But this had long been true in the American economy—for a century in fact —and new capital equipment and its management had offset the rise in labour costs. Why did it go wrong in 1959? In both democracies, America and Germany, all costs pressed prices up and the monetary authorities sought to counter the inflation by damping down the boom.

Secondly, however, *how* did 'the others'—in particular the leaders, Britain and France—get out of the 1948-58 inflationary race? And could they hope to stay out if America and Germany got into a new one? Britain and France had at long last managed in 1957-59 to call a halt to inflation by time-honoured but drastic discipline of their monetary systems. But their currencies remained fixed in official rates or relationships with the US dollar (based on gold at $35.00 to the fine ounce) and through that with German marks, Swiss francs, and all other currencies in fixed exchange rates with the dollar.

So, thirdly, if the price-levels in America and/or Germany for things in normal demand rose faster than those of France and/or Britain—*i.e.* if dollars and/or marks depreciated in purchasing power faster than francs and/or sterling—trade would turn away from things priced in dollars and marks, and it would increase in things priced in francs and pounds. If the countries' price-levels were not kept in line with the fixed exchange rates between their currencies—*i.e.* if each government did not keep the relationship between money and things in its country (its price-level) broadly in step with that relationship in the other countries—the fixed, official exchange rates between those countries' currencies could not possibly be maintained. If American or German prices in general soar, while British and French prices don't, world traders will buy in Britain and France the things which all four countries can offer, rather than in America or Germany. So to keep trade for their own industries and workers the Americans and Germans will have to cheapen dollars and marks: will have to devalue them, to quote more of them than before to sterling and francs. That is what Britain, France, and all other former inflaters had to do earlier in the post-war period.

And so, fourthly and finally, since Britain and France earlier, and America and Germany later, seem to run headlong into such difficulties because of inflation, is it not probable that the causes lie not in mere monetary matters but rather in politics and society? Is it not more probable that the monetary *manifestations* of inflation—soaring price-levels, rising interest rates, flights from fixed-interest bonds into variable (and hence rising) dividend-yielding equity shares, and so on—are really symptoms of a disease to which democracies seem peculiarly prone? Is it *because* they are democracies?

The currency relationships and arrangements established at Bretton Woods in 1944 between the leading, world-trading, industrial democracies ensure one thing at any rate. Inflation continued as a policy in any of them must either draw the rest along, or force the inflater to devalue his own currency as against all the others. So many democracies have (a) followed inflation as a policy since 1945, (b) at differing national rates, (c) have consequently had to devalue their currencies (many of them more than once in a decade), (d) ending up with America and Germany (long the soundest) threatening to go the same inflationary way, that (e) we may well suspect some cause built into democracy itself, or at any rate into modern industrial democracies run by representative governments elected by universal adult suffrage.

Economic Convulsions in Democracies

Democracies are now confined to Western Europe, North America, and to isolated industrial societies elsewhere, like Japan, South Africa, and Australia. All of them, without exception, have shown—most of them show—the same inflationary manifestations. All of them are supposed to concert their monetary policies in order to keep up a steady rate of growth in international trade (full employment), to maintain a general international stability of prices, and to preserve their currencies' mutual official values in other currencies (the exchange rates) through the international institutions of the United Nations and of the International Monetary Fund set up in Washington after the conference at Bretton Woods in 1944.

Remarkable, in view of world events since 1945, as has been

the general level of success in the international achievement of these aims, success inside each separate industrial democracy has not been so remarkable. And in, and therefore between, all of them inflation has taken tolls, caused devaluations, and been pursued as a policy at varying national rates. The effects upon the different industrial democracies have consequently varied; but the combined effect of so many varying national inflations on the economic development of the free half of the world has been to make its progress spasmodic, convulsive and unreliable.

The turnabout of the United States between 1949 and 1959 is sorry testimony—from the confident, freely-trading, generous, stable, economic saviour of the democratic half of the world, to the apprehensive, more protectionist, more careful, more inflationary, economic portent to the other democracies today. Almost as sad testimony is borne by Germany. She is now—like America —so much richer than in 1949, and possessed of so much of the gold and other reserves which America has meanwhile lost, yet fighting (like America) the same built-in inflation at home, but behaving in the foreign economic field in no way like the good American creditor of mankind a decade earlier.

Alongside these, which are two of the strongest economic systems among industrial democracies, we can range Britain, France, and the others whose post-war progress for a decade and a half has been one long inflation punctuated by crises and devaluations. As the 1960s opened, neither they—nor any other democracies—showed much disposition to face the international problem of continuing national inflations: some causal, some consequential, all of them carried along together, none of them stopped.

In the free half of the world alone vestigial democracy, representative government, consumers' and producers' choices, private enterprise, and personal freedoms remained. But instead of facing the unfree, authoritarian half with steady, co-ordinated, economic growth, progressive yet settled societies, and dependable co-operation between them, the leading, free nations contrived to present a social and economic picture almost as arbitrarily convulsive and spasmodic as that presented by the Communist half of the world. Whereas the Communist half produced its convulsions by lack of fundamental freedoms and by authoritarian plans for the future, the free half produced its spasms by unco-ordinated inflations and consequent interferences with the working out of those freedoms. There was more than met the eye of each half-world's system in the other.

Democracy's Economic Advantage

'But surely,' the innocent non-economist will object, 'all you are saying about inflation in and by modern industrial democracies amounts to advocacy of totalitarianism: an extraordinary argument by a freedom-loving, libertarian individualist.' Neither true; nor extraordinary if it were. First, because if it were true, a lover of truth more than liberty (if those were ever by their nature opposed) ought to tell it, as he sees it, though the heavens fall. And secondly, because Communist, Socialist and other 'totalitarian democracies' (Professor Y. Talmon's phrase) do *not* successfully avoid inflation and its real burdens upon a people. They are only very successful in the masking, redistribution, and gerrymandering of those real burdens. At least as long as any democracy endures, the effects of inflation can be seen and acted upon.

The remaining democracies must still allow certain facts to come to light. They must still leave a sector of the economy to free and competitive private enterprises. Personal, private and corporate possessions of money and other property are still not 100 per cent controlled by State authorities. Foreign trading is still open. So despite all State controls over and interventions in the economy, natural prices and costs for most things, reached by the free and competitive 'higgling of the market' (Adam Smith), come to light. The democratic State can nationalize this and that industry, set up monopoly after monopoly, clap many trades and economic pursuits in State-tailored strait-waistcoats, and so rig demands and supplies and markets and prices. But money itself remains, and can be privately exchanged for goods. Some indication of 'natural' values, of costs and prices therefore remains, relating to all kinds of goods and services. So the effects of inflation on all of them emerge and can be traced and talked about.

As long as a fair amount of personal and corporate freedom remains to do as one wishes with one's own money and other private property, people will eye the trend in the purchasing power of money and all other trends dependent on it, and dispose of their money and property to what they deem their best advantage. Hence the awareness of inflation's effects in democracies. Hence, too, the problems created by the economic activities of property-owning persons, which inflating democratic States increasingly try to bring under controls. And hence, finally, the compulsion upon an inflating democratic State to undo democracy.

The Totalitarian Economy

But in a 100 per cent Socialist State or Commonwealth the production, distribution, exchange and uses of everything—manpower, materials, machines, transport, work-space—are decreed, and compelled to occur as closely as possible 'according to plan'. The calculations and measuring are done by money and credit because that is the only way to run a modern, highly capitalistic industrial society effectively (if not efficiently).[1] But prices and costs for everything in money do not openly emerge in free markets by competitive enterprise. There is neither producers' nor consumers' choice. The plans and their execution are actually conceived in *non*-monetary terms, almost in those of primitive barter: so many thousand tons of this, so many thousand man-hours necessary to a task, so many freight carloads, so many houses—and all (naturally) of standard kinds to achieve the plans.

Accordingly when production does not work out, or quality and standards fall—as they do for both human and superhuman reasons in the life of a nation or of many nations, due to bad harvests or new discoveries or epidemics or cussedness—the execution of the totalitarian State's original plans, supervised by a large and costly bureaucracy watching every detail, must still appear to ensue. It cannot be allowed to appear to fail, as that would mean a continuous scrapping of plans: planning to be unplanned. Consequently arbitrary, forceful alterations have continuously to be made to the various human or material ingredients, and to the standards or qualities as well. Thus, the 100 per cent totalitarian Socialist State achieves its plans not always, but mainly, on time; but certainly not up to standard, specification, quality, or durability.

[1] See Chapter 4, p. 55.

A massive rigidity and cumbrousness are caused by planning and undertaking important economic operations in real terms by State bodies. But the people do not know the relative values of things. The massive bureaucracy need not publish its money-accounts, as long as the plans appear to be fulfilled. The true costs of production, the true costs of errors, need never be published. Only crises occur within the bureaucracy.

Not leaving such decisions and operations to free enterprise, public markets, and the automatic measuring and registering of results in money costs and prices, necessarily does away with democracy and freedoms. It gives the State the power to inflate, to force savings from the masses and to make them produce and consume what they are told to, for the good of the State's plans. It gives the State, therefore, the power to cover up the real costs of inflation. They are covered in the general, massive loss of efficiency, or slower rate of consumers' progress, or social and political tensions, or absence of many things the consuming masses would prefer to what the State produces. But it also does away with the priceless democratic boon of the finest, most accurate, most sensitive and automatic economic measuring instrument for all values: the natural costs and prices of everything in free and competitive markets.

Great as is the rate of growth in the scientific and material achievements of 100 per cent totalitarian States, they have not been achieved by inflation as a policy. On the contrary—and the significance of this fact alone should be realized by all democrats —the published discussions among economists and other technical experts in totalitarian States show that their advice has ever been to avoid inflationary effects, although those effects would only work out in real and not in money terms, in the private world of bureaucrats' statistics and not in public, and unperceived by the masses of consumers. Most significantly, the political rulers of Russia have consistently tried to follow their advice. They realized their achievements, plans and aims depended alike on the highest possible efficiency.

It is a pity that an even higher degree of economic efficiency —that of finer calculations by sound money, free markets and competitive enterprise—was impossible for the totalitarian rulers because their political doctrine ranked above it. It was also a pity that the political rulers of democracies strove so hard to copy the totalitarians' means of massively covering up the effects and costs of inflation, without making sure they avoided the thing itself as well as the totalitarians avoided it.

Democracy's Disadvantages

The weaknesses of a totalitarian State are great but concealed. Those of a democracy are perhaps not so great but paraded. On the whole the latter is the preferable State, for it is publicly remediable.

The built-in weakness of a democracy—and it has always been so—is its proneness to pressure from vested economic group-interests. These latter seek specially advantageous treatment from representative governments in return for their votes. The more equal the opposing political party forces in a democracy, the greater the temptation—the less resistible—to angle for the votes of these organized vested interests. Their votes, as in ancient Athens or Rome, go with their pressure. Their pressure is exerted on governments for their own specific, peculiar, particular, material gain. Taxes, tariffs, subsidies, rewards for public servants, costs of State services—these are the more obvious means of sectional material advantage. They are used to benefit such pressure-groups by weak democratic governments at the cost of the whole society or of those large parts of it who pay the enhanced taxes, tariffs, subsidies, and prices of State services.

Thus a great part of the national income—which is the national output—becomes a happy hunting ground for raids by democratic governments in favour of booty for privileged pressure-groups: and this at a time when the days of privilege and class are supposed to have been superseded by democracy itself. Such material corruption of the spirit of democracy, such perversion of its principles and practices alike, pervades the Left as much as the Right, agriculture as much as industry, management as much as trade unions, and officers of the State as much as ordinary citizens.

In all economic groupings—agriculture, industry, distributive trades, clerical and professional occupations, State industries and services, and the State's own bureaucracy itself—the corruption of political pressure for sectional material gain unites, rather than divides, the two older and opposed sectionalisms of employers' vested interests and those of employees. In the modern

118

industrial democracy the political pressure of trade unionists as organized workers for their own sectional gain is more frequently and publicly expressed than that of employers' associations: to prevent free competition at home or abroad, to keep out (or discharge if it is 'in') any refugee or other foreign labour, to limit apprenticeship or training, to stop new machines or methods operating at their productive best (*i.e.* to stop their lowering of unit costs and prices). On the employers' side, collective arrangements to keep up prices, to keep out foreign competitors, to keep away home competition, and to secure sectional levies, tolls, or subsidies also exert pressure upon parliaments and parties. Often the employers' and trade unions' pressures on governments coincide, at society's cost; and when the State is the employer—as in all nationalized industries and services—they always coincide.

Such pressures need not be—often are not—overt, formal and deliberate. The weaker, lazier, more timid and more apprehensive the government and the parties opposed to it, the more naturally and automatically do they succumb to the temptation to buy votes, to give in to the pressure-groups before the latter even formulate demands, to make sure of electoral support from such sectional vested interests at the public's expense and to 'head-off trouble' by favouring them in advance, so earning their political gratitude ahead of any need to do so. Geographical sections of the country ply their sectional interests along with economic groupings. Whole industries and occupations seek material benefits at a weak democratic government's and opposition's hands. What the entire community, the society, does not see and can barely feel in economic terms is easily and speedily voted by such parliaments in favour of a clamant few who are loudly willing to 'stand up and be counted'. The costs are there, but are paid by the unorganized electors. They are so widely spread that they can be well concealed.

In this way the so-called Welfare State—the system of State-organized and distributed welfare at the forced expense of contributors and higher-tax payers—also becomes a happy hunting ground for political raids. Benefits, pensions, subsidies to families or other consumers tend to be decided with as much of an eye to the next election result as to what is sound for the national economy, or as to what is sound even for the beneficiaries whose marginal votes loom so large in the political arithmetic of timid or calculating democrats. Thus taxes and other State levies on individuals and businesses rise to penal heights but still fail to balance soaring Budgets. Budgets already overloaded by State expenditure are then nominally covered by inflation.

Rather than risk unpopularity in the eyes of any grouping and bring State expenditure and taxes down in parallel, leaving the citizenry to perform more welfare and other economic activities for themselves, democratic governments and oppositions alike prefer to cover gaps in State expenditure by inflation. So State spending can never fall. Similarly they prefer to find the extra money and credit in the same inflationary way to buy off threatened strikes in State industries, to enable whole private industries to pay any and every wage demand and keep up full employment, and to keep in profitable being even the inefficient firms by inflationary easy money for easy profits. It is little wonder that in face of such bi-partisan timidity and inflationary easy-goingness more and more electors in modern industrial democracies become more and more uncertain which is which— government and opposition, Right and Left. That has at any rate been the common experience of almost all West European democracies since 1945.

It explains those equally confusing reversals of traditional rôles in the democracies, due to post-war obsession with 'full employment policies'—the preference of trade unionists for longer hours (at overtime rates) rather than leisure, the raising under Socialism of the British tariff (with the support of trade unions and employers' associations) to one of the highest in the world, the use of other State controls to ensure work in established if obsolescent trades at no matter what cost (full employment) rather than transference to new trades, and the keeping up of all costs and prices by protectionism, subsidies, and other arthritic State artifices aimed at full employment, no matter in what direction or at what rate the stiffened economy might then have to move. The general democratic preoccupation with work rather than leisure, with sectional producers rather than the body of consumers, and with everyday expediency rather than sound principles, has led to such confusion in politics and economics that the very system of representative and parliamentary government has rapidly come into common contempt.

Symptoms of Inflation as a Policy

Such conduct by the State, under democratic governments of differing (and of all) parties, naturally results in the classic manifestations of perpetual inflation. We have described *indexisation* of government bonds in France and elsewhere—the guaranteeing of a *real* rate of future yield on the bonds if inflation proceeds (by tying the yield to the price of gold) instead of only a fixed nominal rate of interest. But in Britain and other usually more stable democratic societies even Conservative governments felt themselves forced, by the growing public distrust of the currency's future purchasing power, to introduce such unheard-of devices (to circumvent distrust of the fixed rates of interest on their bonds) as the offer of big capital bonuses on gilt-edged after seven years (free of tax) and 'Premium Bonds' based on a lottery (the premia drawn by lot being also non-taxable). They even felt forced in social fairness to change the laws governing investments in trustee securities (mainly 'gilt-edged' or their equivalent, at fixed interest). This was so that trustees, like other folk, could 'hedge' against perpetual inflation, by investing their beneficiaries' funds in equities yielding dividends likely to rise in the inflationary future, and therefore saleable in that future at higher prices for a capital gain (not taxable).[1]

All these and other all-party, official, belated actions in industrial democracies are really recognitions of inflation as a policy. Most of them have been brought in by Conservative, Centre, or Right-wing governments. Ready to stem too-rampant inflation for a year or so, they yet go thus far in admitting their inability —or refusal—to stem it, singly or together with other democratic governments, as a policy for the future. And to the Left of Centre in these democracies the apostles of collectivism and complete State *dirigisme* propose to do likewise, faster, but with even higher penal taxation, more personal and business unfreedom, and a capital gains tax to scoop into the hands of the inflating State the paper gains of all taxpayers, which might have helped to preserve their property and its original value. This latter tax thus becomes a capital levy by the State. It recognizes that inflation is running democracy's capital down, not building it up.

The limits of personal and corporate toleration in an inflating democracy are soon reached, as long as freedoms remain. Driven

[1] See Chapter 5, p. 75.

to bribe electors in one vested interest after another by fear of losing power, eager to seem beneficent with public money on all sides, but aware that its policies and practices have driven citizens beyond those limits and in so doing have begun to undo democracy, the government both inflates and tries to control inflation's results in despair. It is open confession that the arbitrary, inequitable, and massive 'forced saving' of inflation becomes inevitable in democracy if its governments are bankrupt of convictions and courage. It is open confession that democracy cannot endure under government by expediency; under government that coasts along on tides of bribery from the public purse. Under sound, bold leadership—even in the most critical times and predicaments, and even against wide unpopularity—democracy can endure, adapt, and spring back where authoritarian systems crack, collapse and are superseded. But it has never endured under followership.

CHAPTER 8

DEMOCRATIC AND TOTALITARIAN GROWTH

The chief economic aim in the modern world, both in industrialized and not-yet-industrialized countries, is rapid growth: the development of more economic resources in every country as rapidly as possible. This problem has been dramatized for the world by the Russian economic challenge to the United States: a peaceful challenge to 'competitive co-existence' in Mr Krushchev's own words. Yet that competition is between two great nations, rather two economic and political systems, both already reposing on enormous industries and disposing of much productive capital per man. Their economic *means*, their methods of production, are almost identical; but the social *ends* of all that production differ enormously.

Americans remain wedded to a time-honoured Western social philosophy of individual and corporate freedoms. It stems from John Locke through Adam Smith ('the sole end of production is consumption') to the Sherman-Clayton anti-trust laws and the New Deal legislation of the 1930s. These laws built a framework within which competitive private enterprises, free markets and consumers' choices can turn out what consumers want (or can be persuaded they want), while the individual American citizen's personal liberties are guaranteed and preserved as nowhere else West or East (save only Switzerland). The Federal Government and those of the 50 States in the American Union have, and exercise, only such powers of intervention in conditions of business and economic life as are deemed necessary to preserve law and order, to safeguard the competitive framework abovementioned, and to provide a minimum of basic economic services for all individual and corporate persons (*e.g.* defence, highways, sanitation, unemployment insurance, posts, public hygiene, standards of service in food, pharmaceutical, and other trades 'affected with the public interest', etc). All else is left to competitive private enterprise, which in turn depends for its capital on profits and on competition for any other available savings of individual and corporate persons.

The Russian system reverses this order of things. Almost all economic activity is determined *a priori* by plans into which all must fit, and only an insignificantly small sector is left free to private initiative. Jobs, new investments, production, consumption, even savings, are all decreed beforehand, and then have to work out 'according to plan'. Whether they do so work out or not is immaterial to 'the system' in one sense: namely, that if they do not, the execution of the plan is arbitrarily varied to make them do so later on, and the time for the fulfilment of the whole plan is extended, no matter how high the cost. This necessitates the extension of the hand of the State into almost every sector of human life, both individual and corporate.

A fully Socialist system is automatically, necessarily and almost exhaustively one of State controls over all aspects of individual and associational life, exercised through a hierarchy of bureaucrats, from the highest levels of responsibility and income to the lowest. Only by such comprehensive State controls, and by such arbitrary decisions, costs, and modifications can the predetermined figures of 'economic growth' in the plan be achieved. That this system works—that its achievements in terms of rapid growth in the basic capital equipment of a modern industrial State can be dramatic—only a fool would deny. But that in its (in any case heavy) costs must not only be reckoned monumental wastes but also massive personal inhumanities and unfreedoms, only Western 'fellow-travellers' deny. Official Russian literature admits them.

The rest of the nations of the world look on at this *confrontation* of two social systems, now vowed not only to peaceful coexistence but also to economic competition. Those of Asia, Africa and Latin America who have not yet decided to follow 'the American way' or the Russian, await developments. They await the outcome of the race in economic growth between the two giants, West and East. In between come, uneasily—more socialized than the Americans and more dependent for their rates of growth on competitive private enterprise than the Russians—the remaining Western democracies in Europe and other continents. They are what economists call, without international irony, 'mixed economies'. Some, like Britain, France, or Sweden, are more mixed with State economic activities than others, like Western Germany, Belgium and Japan. They all 'lie a little farther off' from 'the American way' and a little farther off from the Russian way. Their citizens' personal and corporate freedoms are more State-regulated by bureaucracy than those of Americans; less so than those of Russians. The initiative and competitiveness of their private enterprises are not as marked—because they are not as assured and safeguarded by as strict a legislative framework—as those of Americans.

Investment for Growth

The chief problem in securing economic growth—and one becoming more acute as growth is needed more rapidly—is to secure the savings, the foregone consumption of immediately available resources, which must be invested in new productive capital equipment. Clearly a totalitarian system can secure such savings, and therefore such growth, more rapidly than a democratic system—*provided* its State compulsion and ubiquitous unfreedom do not prove too costly in unproductive bureaucracy, policing powers, and economic errors due to the rigidities and inflexibilities of 'planning' (to say nothing of social crises, 'going slow' by disappointed and cowed worker-consumers, and possibly civil strife). That is because such a totalitarian State can now hold down standards of consumption, compel saving, decree hours of work and leisure, freeze jobs, etc, in an all-embracing manner utterly impossible in the ancient world. So what was impossible to Diocletian is possible to Mr Krushchev.

But clearly also a democratic system—for instance that of the United States since 1917 and despite two World Wars and a world slump—can record rates of economic growth, standards of production and consumption, and amounts of investment in new capital per worker, and in *all* manufacturing, agricultural, and service industries, such as Russia has still very far to go to equal.

'Mixed economies' run the risk of getting the worst, not the best, of both the giant economic systems, East and West. For these two giant systems are 'pure'. They run on unitary, consistent, articulated lines. And one disturbing pointer is worth noting. The Russian and other totalitarian States have avoided inflation while securing rapid economic growth by the simple method of forcibly slashing consumption to secure the necessary savings. They have done this in many ways—not allowing production of a whole range of consumers' goods familiar to every Western home, or producing them only for export, or arbitrarily altering wages, or equally arbitrarily altering the domestic purchasing power of their money (the price-level) and by a host of other and simultaneous measures.

In other words the totalitarians have played the game of rapid economic growth strictly according to the rules of the classical economists down to Lord Keynes: no matter how much new investment in productive capital was decreed within a given period, the *real savings* for it (*i.e.* the exactly equal amount of currently available resources) were withdrawn from immediate consumption, and inflation was thereby, at least for most of the time, strikingly avoided. That it was so avoided by force, unfreedoms and personal illiberties does not invalidate the economic principle which they respected: namely, that if you try to invest in new capital equipment within a given period *more* resources than your people are prepared voluntarily, or can be compelled by the State, to save from their current production, all prices will get out of gear and inflation will result. The totalitarians have signally avoided it, while securing rapid growth in their basic, primary, productive capital.

On the other hand the not-quite-so 'pure' American economic system (it is itself more 'mixed' than the totalitarian) functions efficiently in securing rapid economic growth. But not without inflationary, and sometimes deflationary, 'hiccups' now and then. These must be set against the personal and associational freedoms guaranteed by 'the American way'; just as the rigid consistency, articulation, and therefore 'purity' (almost Puritanicalness) of the totalitarian system, *without* inflation, must be set against the high personal and associational cost of illiberties and unfreedoms.

The 'Mixed Economy' Lags

Why, and how, is it, then, that the West European and other (*e.g.* Australian) industrialized democracies have contrived certainly since 1917, and even since 1945, both to lag in economic growth compared with America and Russia, and to secure such growth as they have achieved with far greater degrees of inflation and of inflationary social troubles? There is one obvious answer. Their economies are more 'mixed', less 'pure' and consistent, than the Russian and American systems. Their State activities in the economic field hamper, constrain, and circumscribe their private enterprises, and compete with them for available savings. State and private business seldom pull together, and often pull apart, in the 'mixed economies' ' effort for economic growth. There is no rigid Russian planned system in them; neither is there a fully flexible, competitive, free enterprise system—not as much as the American system can still show.

The disadvantages of both the giant Eastern and Western systems—the State rigidities, and the erratic economic ups-and-downs due to a 'pull Devil, pull baker' between State activities and private enterprises—combine in the West European and other democratic 'mixed economies' to hold back economic growth. Limits to such growth are built into these democratic 'mixed economies' by the perpetual clash between State activities and the needs of private enterprise. Then the State, by the political action of governments, seeks the easier but temporary solution of creating money and credit to 'buy time' as well as to buy-off the opposition of threatened vested interests (those of workers in trade unions as well as those of employers, users of State services, pensioners, etc, etc). It prefers this to the harder but durable solution of attracting and ensuring enough savings of all kinds, by persons and companies, to match the new investment needed for a given rate of economic growth. Inflation, again, is seen as the outcome of lazy, timid, yet democratic government. And as long as such inflationary 'solutions' to the tug-of-war between State activities and private enterprises persist—as they are bound to persist, being only temporary—inflation becomes built-in and progressive.

The democratic State with a mixed economy is forced to control and regulate private persons and businesses progressively. It is forced, having unleashed inflation, to cover up its effects. It tries to remove the symptoms by new State controls, new regulations, and new laws about the *minutiae* of personal and corporate life, rather than to remove the disease. And thus democracy undoes itself by creating an increasingly compulsive, restrictive bureaucracy, upon which everyone and everything increasingly come to depend for permits, nods, and so-called initiatives. In the end democratic Parliaments see their own freedom vanish with the value of the currency, and a centralized bureaucracy reigns. A centralized State socialism comes about *malgré* governments, oppositions, and citizenry—*malgré* even the Socialists, for they would prefer to bring about their ideal economy by a safer road.

The fallacy that you can control inflation in a democracy through bureaucratic controls over prices, production and trade persists among us today. But only symptoms are removed; the lady has her double-chin removed by surgery, only to discover it at the back of her neck. The State—today or in history—merely removes one symptom and replaces it with another; favours a new class of person by inflation, while penalizing another; or, in attempting to regulate social and economic life while persisting with inflation, runs the machinery of democratic government, the currency itself, and the entirety of social law and order headlong into catastrophe.

Such a situation occurred twice in our lifetime in Germany (after both world wars). It proceeded far in France. And in Britain the pound sterling lost *nearly one-half of its purchasing-power in the 14 post-war years alone*. It is idle for democratic governments to imagine that such an inflationary situation—and all its social consequences—can ever be cured by letting inflation continue while suppressing its manifestations.

Inflation and Social Dynamics

There is, moreover, an interesting and important relationship between persistent inflation and what we may call social growth or dynamics. It does not appear from the classic inflations that inflation and economic dynamics go together. It does not appear that to get rapid economic expansion you *must* inflate. It does not appear that to get 'full employment' you have to put up with inflation. On the contrary, the classic inflations in history have redistributed whatever capital or wealth had already been accumulated. Thus they gave a big boost to consumption—for instance, in early Imperial Rome, in Europe between 1525 and 1650, and between 1945 and 1958 in Britain. Such inflations seem, therefore, to spell prosperity at least to many consumers, at the cost of a minority of former capital owners. They even transform the nature of capital itself. For instance, they made land and farms more valuable than town houses after the flight from the cities 'back to the land' in the later Roman Empire, just as they have recently made farms, real estate, works of art, and equity shares relatively more valuable, more worthwhile to hold, than money, bank deposits, or Government bonds.

These inflations more often seem to have spelled a secular decline; or to have spelled social and economic statics rather than dynamics. They certainly made some rapid social changes, but not in the direction of a general, durable, material betterment for the entire society. Rather the reverse: they ran society down, tore it apart. Even in Britain and West Germany after World War II the striking rise in standards of consumption for the mass of people only came about by redistributive taxation, or else *after* inflation was deliberately checked by their Governments. It did not come about by the rapid growth of productivity *during an inflation.*

The converse of this is that if you look for technical and material progress, a period of real social and economic dynamics, you will more often find it—as economists would expect—when more and more *new* capital is created, when interest rates are high, when big investment opportunities exist, when money seems to enjoy enough stability and reliability of purchasing-power in the present and future to enable risks to be assessed and incurred for calculable prices, and when possessors of money incomes can measure the comparative attractions of spending on immediate consumption or investing for an equally reliable future yield. Such lasting periods of material progress and dynamic advance were found pre-eminently in the eighteenth and nineteenth centuries; and (more recently) in West Germany and France after their post-war currency reforms, and in Britain after the Government's eventually severe monetary measures in 1957. As a corollary, the economic dynamics of American society were at their peak when the dollar's purchasing-power was more stable than that of other nations' currencies.

The Inflationary Trilemma

The more productive capital a democratic society needs, the more inflation will drive that society on to a three-horned trilemma. It will have to abandon freedom and secure savings forcibly, so long as inflation persists; or it will have to abandon inflation to get the savings voluntarily in a democratic society; or it will have to slow down or abandon economic progress and the necessary rate of formation of capital, if it remains democratic but inflates.

In history we do not witness such a trilemma until modern times, when productive capital per head becomes great. But it is interesting to note the decline of standards, as inflation persisted, in ancient and modern inflations alike. The supply of slaves—the ancient equivalent of our modern machines and other capital—ran out. Capital consumption was hectic and general. Mobile assets disappeared—particularly the slaves, and even a great number of the free citizens. In more modern times, because inflation benefits all debtors and penalizes creditors, progressive inflation—inflation as a policy—militates against the very process of capital-formation on which material progress, social dynamics and technological advances in a democracy depend.

The inflating modern democratic State faces this trilemma, which bears repetition. It must abandon individual and social freedoms if it is both to form new capital fast enough and to inflate. It must abandon inflation if it is both to conserve freedoms and to form capital fast enough. Or it must abandon hopes of rapid material progress (new capital formation) if it is both to inflate and to conserve individual freedoms. I need say no more about the ways this trilemma presents itself to us in the world today—as between Russia and the West, as between democratic governments and their citizens, as between (say) the United States and Britain inflating at different rates, as between developed and under-developed countries, as between debtors and creditors both national and international, as between saving or investment on the one hand and spending or consumption on the other, as between all who still work and can raise their earnings and those who have retired on fixed money incomes and cannot. We have experience of all these things.

Never have the nations of the world been so short of capital simultaneously. Never have they tried to progress materially so fast in all quarters. Never have there been so many simultaneous inflations, but at differing rates, putting such high premiums on consumption and such penalties on savings. The rule we discerned in the inflations of history is clearly observable at work today. The more inflation is persisted in (or allowed to persist) as a policy, the more do democratic governments undo with their left hand what they strive to do with their right. Inflation is thus the parent of paradox.

Inflation and Politics

Not the least of paradoxes today—in politics and in economics —is that great masses of people in the democracies, in America, Germany, France or Britain, begin to understand what inflation means. They act on the assumption that it must be reckoned with, hedged against, evaded. They begin to treat it as a weapon aimed at them, whether directly by the State or by the sellers of goods and services. So Governments—like the French two or three years ago—can only borrow 'long' by pegging their bonds to gold; or employers and employed make bargains in the light of an already-discounted rate of future depreciation of the money.

When this awareness of inflation as a built-in social institution becomes general, the advantages of inflation to the State, the bureaucracy, the trade unions, and the State-centralizing political party (or parties) begin to fade away. The end is in sight. Something like this accounts for the extraordinary apathy and absenteeism during recent British elections. In Britain recently, in the wake of inflation, big blocks of normally faithful Socialist voters did not go out and vote, partly because the Labour Party's promises and its record seemed to prove it unwilling to halt a twenty-year-old inflation. Such an attitude is dangerous for democracy, but symptomatic. It is a strange reaction to the Labour Party's official denigration of, and contempt for, 'sound money', profits, 'the bankers', and 'the City'.

Here are social effects of inflation a-plenty. Again a paradox emerges. Modern society depends more and more on the increase of productive capital per head. Yet, in the name of welfare for all, many of the leading industrial nations of the world have moved steadily away from sound money and voluntary savings and democratic freedoms, towards more and more force and compulsion, exercised through an oligarchy of bureaucrats. At the same time, Conservatives and Socialists protest that they are both anti-Communist, anti-totalitarian. Surely if we can only progress materially by compulsion of a monolithic State apparatus—if all the mobility of capital and labour, of saving and spending, that we can enjoy is what the State will allow us, and if all of this apparatus is clamped down on us because of the attempts of the inflating State to cover up symptoms rather than to cure a disease—we ought to look far more closely at the disease. We ought to begin by asking the old question *Cui bono?* Whom does inflation benefit? As of old, the answer will come back: the State itself, the bureaucracy, the Government, the political set-up—not even those who work as against those who do not. Inflation comes from, and by, lazy, timid government. That is why it is such a threat to a free society.

Viewed dispassionately and superficially, the modern world in any case does not seem to have much time or much room for democracy, representative government or a free society. They have not taken root, or if they once did they have soon been uprooted, over most of the earth; and even in the British Commonwealth they seem on the defensive. Much of this is due to widespread misconceptions about economic issues, and in particular about 'full employment' and inflation.

In the remaining democracies run by representative governments, 'full employment', the goal of social action after 1945, has come to be identified with 'every worker's job guaranteed to him'. More, the phrase has come to mean to the worker 'my job should last as long as I want it to, without any changes unless I want them, and I need never move to another job in another place unless I want to'. It also came to mean easy paper profits for unenterprising employers. Thus, in another paradox, 'full employment', which in wartime had been conceived as a stimulus to peacetime progress and a dynamic society, turned out to be a potent factor making society static, conserving out-of-date industries and methods, protecting inefficiencies, and positively putting a premium upon inflexibility. Instead of resourceful suppleness, enterprise, and adaptability, democratic society in the 'mixed economies' got a kind of economic rheumatoid arthritis. Instead of high mobility from old to new, from declining to advancing industries, it got rigidity and ossification in the old and declining industries but no healthy bankruptcies of the inefficient. Loud economic and political demands were made upon democratic governments to shield, buffer and protect every conceivable economic interest vested in those naturally declining industries. Few governments withstood them.

Far and away the worst example was agriculture throughout the highly industrialized West. And the worst case of all was North American agriculture. In the USA and Canada, both highly industrialized States with politically powerful *blocs* of farmers, the agriculture of last century was protected in the middle of this century, and even stimulated to produce further surpluses, by guaranteed prices to the farmers. The prospering townsfolk paid in taxes and the retail prices of food to keep far too many farmers not only at standards of life comparable to those set by manufacturing in the towns and cities, but also to preserve every farmer and every farm in work. Surpluses piled up until special prefabricated containers had to be bought to house them, although they were being given away to needy nations. They were 'dumped' overseas, upsetting normal markets and trading, much of it the trade of the same under-developed nations to whom the North American surpluses were later to be given. The problem has never been solved. It abides with us now. And what was so blatantly uneconomic in North America was just as uneconomic in Germany, France, Britain, Belgium, etc (though neither so blatant nor so obvious) where it continues unsolved.

Instead of the free world's trade being expanded by the regular growth of international 'give and take' in product after product —the under-developed countries raising their export earnings by selling more agricultural and primary products to the developed West, and the West in turn exporting more capital goods to develop the under-developed countries—this natural flow of world trade has been impeded. It still is impeded, largely in and by the Western industrial countries themselves where 'full employment', industrial and agrarian protectionism, and inflation have alike been so pronounced and so continuous since 1945.

Even the recent moves by groups of mainly industrial nations in Europe to free industrial trade *among themselves*—by the Six Powers of the European Economic Community and the Seven of the European Free Trade Area—exempt their domestic, protected agriculture from the schemes; make no provision to *generalize* their mutual and reciprocal concessions for the good of countries outside Europe; and bid fair to stimulate still more the considerable trade in manufactures among themselves alone (already industrialized countries) behind substantial tariffs.

Such settings for *national* 'full employment' of everybody and everything in industrial democracies (at no matter what cost) are not at all what the wartime framers of the United Nations and the International Bank and Monetary Fund had in mind. Lord Keynes and his colleagues—Americans, British and all others—were at any rate of one mind upon these things: that the post-war world would prove unitary in its economic destinies; that its rapid economic progress could only be assured by relative stability of the purchasing-power of all moneys and by dependable relationships between currencies; and that individual nations—at least those already developed and industrialized—would have to secure 'full employment' for their peoples by *international* economic co-operation rather than by reversion to the economic nationalism of 1919-1939.

That earlier inter-war epoch abounded in runaway national inflations, followed by equally runaway national deflations and the consequent world slump and anarchy of 1928-33, all for lack of such international economic co-operation. It was not to occur again.

Yet so hard is international economic co-operation to achieve, and so easy is it to allow national economic affairs to take their own course, that the leading industrial nations of the West since 1945 have, as the war receded, increasingly tended to revert in economic affairs to purely national methods and measures. (Even 'the Six' pursue narrow group interests.) It is scarcely surprising that, in those which remain democracies, inflation persists as a kind of perpetual spectre at the feast.

The True Conditions of Growth

The chief economic problem in modern democratic societies therefore boils down to this: how can such a society secure a rapid and steady rate of economic growth and simultaneously stability of purchasing power in its currency? Clearly the democracies with the most rapidly growing economic systems have as strikingly failed to find a solution as those which are not growing so rapidly: the United States as compared with Britain, Western Germany with Sweden, France with Australia, Italy with Greece, Brazil with Switzerland. This comprehensive failure to reconcile economic growth with reliable money led 'Lombard', the perceptive columnist of the London *Financial Times*, to treat the matter on January 11, 1960, with levity rather than, like other economists, with sorrow. Awarding his own imaginary committee's 'Oscars' for financial performances in the year 1959 he cited:

'The biggest disappointment of the year. The complete failure of the Radcliffe Committee to come forward after a two-year probe of the functioning of the UK's financial system with an attempt at an answer to the major monetary issue of the day—how to devise a monetary policy and back it with other economic controls that would make it possible to combine currency stability with a reasonable and steady rate of progress. . . .

'Best disinflation policy. No award—the committee were unable to find a performance outstanding enough to warrant it.'

His realism, be it noted, came after a year in which most democracies were emerging from two or three years of mild stagnation and had not even yet been caught in another bout of inflationary expansion. Seldom has the democracies' need of *international* co-operation to control national inflationary performances been so clearly manifested.

National programmes for economic growth differ in aims and methods, and there is no necessary harmony or consilience between them. Accordingly, if they depend on or result in persistent inflation, there is no necessary harmony between countries' price levels. But if their currencies are related to each other by fixed exchange rates—$2.80 to £1 to 14 French francs, for example—it is obvious that persistent differences in economic development programmes *and in price-levels* between countries must either force new exchange rates upon governments, or else control over inflation, or else alterations of the development programmes, and possibly all three at once. Hence the devaluation of France, and the devaluations and recurrent crises in the balance of payments of Britain and other democracies, since 1945. That kind of national progress and growth—convulsive, unco-ordinated, disorderly, lopsided and limping—makes hay of any reliable international system of trade and finance. Such an international system becomes more necessary as national industrial systems become more complex and developed.

Hence the Russians' decision after Stalin's death to abandon the 'socialism in one country' principles decreed by him—principles which were used to develop the same socialized industries in Poland, Czechoslovakia, Hungary, etc—in favour of the capitalist 'principles of complementarity', of international specialization, co-operation and reciprocal trading. The international 'conning tower' or economic control office of *Comecon* sees that the plans for economic growth and the financing thereof, the values of moneys, and the foreign trading of the various Socialist States beyond the Iron Curtain keep in step. They do this not only to attain the most rapid common rate of economic growth, but also to preserve the dependability of the various Socialist moneys; for in these all prices, loans, repayments and other economic calculations in transactions (simultaneously or over long periods) are made. In that way, too, they show a more perceptive, cannier, classical economist's respect for the basic principles of capital creation, economic growth, saving and investment: namely, an overriding concern to preserve the value of the currency as a reliable measuring-rod for transactions, and thereby to ensure social justice over long periods of time for savers, borrowers and spenders on capital account.

As in a Socialist State virtually all borrowing, spending and investing on capital account must be in State activities, this Governmental determination to abide by the principles of classical economics is worth pondering by the disarrayed democracies and their citizens. That an absolutely Socialist State exercises its powers and economic controls *by force* over its individual and corporate citizens is beside the point in a discussion of inflation and economic growth. The telling point is that the political controllers of such a Socialist State realize what is vital to the success of their growth programmes, and do not flinch from doing it by force. The true response by the politicians of the democracies is not to say 'It can only be done by force, and we prefer chaos and injustice to force,' but to say 'It can be done by consent, and we will show how social order *and* economic growth can be secured without the social injustices of inflation.' But that takes comprehension, convictions, and the courage of them.

PART IV

WHITHER?

CHAPTER 9

SOUND MONEY, SANE SOCIETY

In the course of 1959 public fear of inflation, and behaviour based on it, became apparent in the leading industrial democracies: in the United States, in Germany, France and Britain. Indeed, the unilateral reduction of the Russian manpower in the armed forces in 1960 was, among other things, an indicator of Mr Krushchev's and his colleagues' anxiety to step up the output of consumers' goods and services, and so to diminish the inflationary and social pressures of too big a saving and investment programme. Gradually the dangers of inflation as an instrument of weak or lazy government are becoming apparent around the world.

The throwing of medium- and long-term government bonds at fixed interest into the discard in one leading industrial country after another is conclusive evidence. As the Radcliffe Committee on money and credit put it in Britain in 1959, 'in so far as people foresee a steady rise of prices of 2 per cent per annum, they will look for a 5 per cent rate of interest instead of 3 per cent.' They might have added, 'and 8 per cent instead of 6 per cent.' The odd position in Britain's market for investible savings was reached in 1959 where the yield on government medium- and long-term bonds (gilt-edged) was far higher than that on good business shares (equities). The level of prices of equities had risen to nearly double that of gilt-edged at the same nominal value because individual and institutional investors—a growing army in industrial countries—reckoned with a continuation of rapid inflation, rapid depreciation of the pound's purchasing power; and equities provide a 'hedge' against such depreciation, by rising profits, prices and yields. No 5 or 6 or even 7 per cent bank rate—which is only a governmental interest rate for 'short' money—will cure such public distrust of a currency. The cure for a long-standing disease cannot be lightning-like. It must have its effect upon people's attitudes to long-term investment at fixed interest, to the safe-guarding of their savings through years to come.

The far-sighted author of *Lombard Street*, Walter Bagehot, saw a century ago that democracy and representative government could only be safeguarded in an industrial age by giving 'the workers' a property stake in the system, a capital stake in a capi-talistic society. Such stakes were first achieved by the ordinary working folk of the United States a generation ago. The move-ment spread, with American industrial methods and the conse-quent American standard of living, to 'the masses' in Britain, Germany, Scandinavia, Holland and Switzerland in the 1950s. It bids fair to encompass those of France, Italy and Japan before long. Indeed there are signs that the Russian workers are to be encouraged to hold private investments which will be safe-guarded for their value in the long run.

Modern communications foster this modern, mass property-owning by wider, simpler exposition of economic issues: radio and television, new publications for 'the masses' of both sexes, new specialist literature on everything from leisure-pursuits to modern equipment for homes or hobbies. Therewith the levels rise for public and private discussion of such important national political and economic issues as inflation, productivity, growth, saving and investment. Therewith, too, the natural behaviour of timid or lazy governments becomes increasingly difficult to 'get away with'. On the other hand the ignorance and indifference of 'the masses' are gradually overcome. Formerly they permitted timid or lazy governments easily to 'get away with' surrenders to successive thrusts from organized pressure-groups, at the cost of others in the society. Such massive ignorance of, and indif-ference to, everything except the individual's own immediate interests is being slowly ground down by new and widening com-munications, new social patterns, more leisure, and the gradual social wear-and-tear due to retirement by the aged with old notions and recruitment of the young with new ideas.

All these social changes, concomitants of technical progress, make it harder for lazy or timid governments to pursue inflation as an instrument of policy. At least they make it harder to 'get away with' inflation *without* the increasingly grave social and political tensions set up by the growing public awareness of its dangers. Pessimists about Western culture, democracy, and the educability of 'the masses' should pause to consider the real lessons of our modern mass-communications. The film did not kill the living theatre: it made it, and made it popular. The gramophone or radiogram did not kill the concert and living performers: it made them, and made them massively popular. Radio and television did not kill reading and going to theatres or concerts or any living spectacle: they made them even more massively popular and stimulated older arts to new achievements.

So, too, in political and economic affairs. Industrial mass-society with its apparatus of mass-culture has not killed, drugged or doped serious public and private debate about its vital problems. It is awakening the mass-public, stimulating its intellectual appetites, and making it infinitely less bamboozlable and bulldozable by authority than it ever was before. It is gradually working, albeit with steady acceleration and cumulative effect, against timid or lazy government. It will get the government, and new social institutions or changes in old ones, which it needs. Time is always on the side of new technique. And all the remarkable new technique in economic affairs today demands smooth and complex social co-operation, steady public administration, sound government, reliable money, and dependable present planning for profitable future performance. Uncertainties and undependabilities of all kinds—of social groups, governmental actions, money and prices, or laws and regulations—are anathema to modern productive techniques, and therefore to growth and progress.

Challenges to Progress

True, time is always on the side of new technique; but that is only another way of saying that time is always on the side of change. Indeed, time is change. We can never contract-out of time or change. In modern industrial societies most of the social and economic challenges are thrown down by man's inventiveness and technical progress, in the face of older ways of thinking and behaving. So established trades, business procedures, employers' interests, ways of living, practices of trades unions, productive methods, governmental procedures, fashions of all kinds—all these are constantly being challenged by new and more economical methods. That is the only way in which mankind has made any material progress.

Yet pressure-groups have been organized in modern industrial society to protect the immediate, temporary, material interests of their members *against* the material interests of all other such groups, and especially against the material interests—and at the expense—of the society as a whole: farmers, trade unions, associations of industrialists, pensioners, motorists, ex-service men, etc. The political pressures exerted by such occupational or social groups drive timid or lazy governments into courses of action requiring public funds to be spent for the group alone. This is bribery or blackmail. It has always been common in democracies. It is a recognized, built-in political procedure in the great American Republic and has long been so. ('Sure he's cheating: it's his deal, ain't it?') It is not unknown, though more easily disguised, in dictatorships. But it is important to see it for what it is.

What it does we have already seen.[1] It is, in fact, a brake upon growth and progress. It is a political premium, at public expense, keeping in artificially payable existence those economic occupations and pursuits which have already been shown, by technical advances, to be obsolete or obsolescent. Such are the industrial democracies' subsidies to their farmers. Such are also the British £30,000,000 fund of taxpayers' money to cushion the obsolescence of the Lancashire cotton industry (first in Britain's industrial revolution two centuries ago); the £250,000,000 of British tax funds to enable the railways to pay poor wages to too many workpeople and provide poor public services as a result; and the regular subsidies of over £100,000,000 a year from tax funds to cover losses and pay surplus labour in State services. Such, too, are the more concealed subsidies from the public's purse in America, Germany and other industrial countries which keep in payable existence what technical progress has shown up as uneconomic units in older trades like agriculture, shipping, mining, industries making textiles, watches and precision tools and many other lines. Such uneconomic activities are thus protected by both external (published) and internal (concealed) tariffs and subventions. The real costs of all such protection of backward, out-of-date, or inefficient occupations is masked by spreading it

[1] See Chapter 7, p. 118.

over the whole community of consumers. And inflation does the same, but without any planned protection of particular groups.

The Cost of Sound Money

If the government of a modern industrial democracy decides to abjure inflation as an instrument of policy, both that government and its people must face inescapable social and economic consequences. These consequences will not be new. They are always there in any case. Under continuous inflation they manifest themselves differently, often masked in a woolly veil of inflated prices. Under sound money and sound government, costs and prices of everything emerge into public awareness as what they are in reality: not as what they seem in money of tottering worth. It is important at the outset to emphasize the value to a democracy—especially to its government, business leaders, and all other technical specialists—of *knowing the real costs* of doing or not doing this, that or the other, in the present or the future, here or there, with these people or those, and with these or those persons' savings and other products.

Accordingly, the abandonment of inflation as a policy by any government will automatically uncover *real* values, costs, and prices—costs of materials and fuels as well as of services and different kinds of human labour. It will unmask economic and technical realities with one hand—an advantage to all planning and progress—while provoking with the other much loud and humanly natural opposition from occupations now indicated as obsolescent or no longer efficient.

There are ways—economic and even economical ways—of dealing wisely and humanely with the often abrupt indications of inefficiency set up by new techniques. It is more economical to install new techniques and let them produce fully up to their enhanced capacity, and to spend tax funds on re-training or re-settling or re-distributing the former units and workpeople for new productive purposes, than to minimize, postpone, or hamstring the working of the latest techniques merely in order to 'protect' the obsolescent units and workers. It is more economical and more efficient to grant regular, openly published subsidies from the public purse to cushion such sudden socially and economically shocking transitions, due to technical advances or unforeseeable conditions, than to rig certain wages or other costs arbitrarily and artificially by legislation and/or inflation. For if a government rigs *some* costs that way, it throws a veil over the real values of the goods or services affected. It thus throws out of truth the relationship between those values and all others. Consequently the users of *all* kinds of labour, fuels, materials and services will be to that extent working in the dark, trying to pierce the veils, and striving to bring their own valuations as near to economic truth as possible.

Inflation only does on a grand and *general* scale what arbitrary, artificial, administrative rigging of *particular* costs does to protect anachronisms and inefficiencies on a petty scale. So it will no more do merely to abjure general inflation and then, when the inevitable squeals arise, to have fearful recourse to a series of petty and particular protective devices at public expense, than to abjure such petty and particular protection of inefficiencies and have recourse instead to a general inflation. Humane cushioning of social shocks caused by man's unforeseeable new techniques or other new conditions is a proper charge upon a progressive and progressing society. But the charge should be temporary, estimated, allocated, published, comparable with all other costs, and should fall on shoulders best able to bear it. It should not be allowed to burden those least able to bear it, by holding up the material progress of the entire community—especially not if 'the masses' in their organizations clamour for the protection of obsolescence and retrogression, as in ignorance and communal indifference they generally do. That is the test of both democracy and its leadership.

On this issue employers, investors, farmers and other persons of property must be as clear as the trade unionists and Socialists whom they so often criticize. In the modern State—as many a leading industrial democracy still learns to its apparent surprise —new vested interests are always being built up as old ones are threatened. Once any interest is vested in an established line of conduct or method of procedure, it is vested alike for employers and employed, for trade association and trade union, for men of property in that line and for men without it, for both capital and income, for Tory and Socialist. Clamour and organized action for protection of such vested interests cut across political party lines. That is why in modern democracies the governments of opposing ideologies are generally at one in surrendering to pressure-groups, abandoning leadership in favour of follower-ship, and falling back upon general inflation as a perpetual temporary expedient to buy time.

Required Realism

Accordingly, if democratic government is to survive by grasping such nettles, by restoring sound money—and through sound money sound economic values and plans for a reliable future—the entire democratic community of employers and employed, men of property and men without it, men of the Right and men of the Left, of town and countryside, of all pressure-groups and of none, must be prepared to face the known and calculable costs of faster material progress. They must realize that no existing investment or property, no trade or calling, no established pattern of social life or behaviour, no way of life or pursuit of leisure can be sacrosanct from the inevitable challenges of advancing technique. Those challenges are being, will increasingly be, accelerated. The social shock of their impact must be minimized here and there, wherever it falls.

Economics, material progress, the accumulation of productive capital, are not everything—even if all in the world want them all at once as quickly as possible, and even though they be the foundation upon which all human development, all realization of the individual's potentialities, must rest. But the true costs of cushioning the impacts of these increasing challenges to established attitudes, ways, ideas and economic interests ought to be measured and published as a duty of democratic government. Those true costs and degrees of humane 'protection' must be openly compared and debated for what they are: namely, the costs of a slower material progress for the entire community than would else be possible. That should be the hallmark of a well-led, educated, modern, industrial democracy as contrasted with a totalitarian State wherein the leaders dare not permit public debate about such alternative valuations. To that extent such a democracy should be able to ensure the most rapid and reliable rate of growth for itself, without meanwhile tearing itself asunder by social stresses and convulsions.

One oft-repeated objection to sound money, and therefore to the abandonment of inflation as a policy, comes very naturally from those who contend that 'only a little' inflation ensures full employment of all resources, a perpetual boom, and the most rapid rate of growth. Apart from the problems of keeping such a perpetual inflation to 'only a little' and avoiding the pitfalls and crises described earlier,[1] this variety of 'full employment policy' masks a multitude of very high *real* costs. They are veiled in the continual inflationary rise of *money* costs: in the depreciation of the currency. The objection, the argument, turns upon these alternatives: whether it is better to keep money sound, thereby making it measure real costs as nearly as possible, and keeping all prices and costs as stable as possible; or whether it is better to let money depreciate.

If money is kept sound and stable, the impacts of challenges due to technical progress or other unforeseeable changes will be seen and felt at once. The costs of cushioning them will be measurable. All consequent economic changes will be public, costed, deliberated, known. The society, and all its lines of economic activity, will adjust to them in full awareness of comparative and alternative costs. Technical economic progress—the efficiency or productivity of *all* ingredients of production (and not of human labour alone)—will then show up as a downward movement in the money costs per unit of output. Where the greater productivity emerges, the costs per unit will fall.

Whether profits then pile up, are distributed and 'ploughed back', or managements reduce selling prices, the fruits of progress will flow out into the community of producers and consumers. The general average price level—the cost of living—can be kept relatively stable by this means. The falling unit costs in the technically more progressive lines, the lines with rising productivity, will offset rising costs in older or less efficient lines of activity. All progress in people's consumption and leisure will then come through stable or rising earnings—in shorter working weeks—spent on more and more goods and services with stable or falling prices. And profits will come from the most rapid possible extension and expansion of consumption: *i.e.* from the swiftest possible increase in turnover.

The 'social cost' of this automatic, stable, swift progress on sound money is the community's ever-readiness to adopt and adapt. Earners and taxpayers contribute from their rising stan-

[1] See especially Chapter 5, p. 73.

dards to cushion the shocks of adoption of new ideas, and of adaptation to new methods, imparted to the minority of workers and installations: much as unemployment insurance, but accompanied by positive re-training and re-establishment schemes.

The apologists for 'only a little', but a regular, inflation fail to meet the objection that their deliberate depreciation of the currency does not indicate where adoption and adaptation should begin. Masking the relative efficiencies of all industries, firms, farms, trades and installations with a spurious, paper profitability, the policy of regular inflation fails to distinguish between comparative efficiencies. It does not force out into the public gaze those economic activities which are uneconomic, as soon as they become so as a result of adoption or adaptation elsewhere. It protracts and protects inefficiency and waste.

Steps to Sanity

Accordingly, abandonment of inflation as a policy is bound to bring awkward decisions forthwith before governments, State agencies, bankers, industrial associations, trades unions, and both individual and institutional investors. During the transition from inflation as a policy to sound money, new social and industrial stresses are bound to arise, as the older tensions diminish. The vested interests built-in by regular inflation—particularly those of the non-adopting, non-adapting, less economical trades, firms, employers, trade unions, etc, and of those threatened by new and more productive methods—will squeal. There will be industrial unrest, and probably strikes, in this disaffected, dis-vested, uneconomic, minority sector of the society. It is idle and wrong to say such a transition from unsound to sound money can be made swiftly, easily and painlessly. It cannot, for we have to do with human beings long presented, at public expense, with a windfall profit: with uncovenanted benefits derived not from their own competitive efficiency but from an inflation dispensed by the hand of the State. Men do not lightly surrender such boons; least of all in a democracy.

But it is only right to point out that—granted the democracy's ability and readiness to draw up 'cushioning' and transitional programmes as described above—the social jolts and jerks caused by the halting of inflation and establishing of sound money need not be grave, widespread, costly or enduring. The costs of such a programme will be measurable, known, and allocatable to this or that trade or occupation. The programme itself will be supervisable, its progress calculable, its costs comparable with its achievements. It could be a permanent agency under the aegis of the State, and devolved into local agencies. The progress of regular inflation, on the other hand, is immeasurably confused and its costs severe but unallocatable.

Finally, the automatic indicating of inefficiencies by sound money in a competitive system of private enterprise bears only upon the minority of trades, occupations and persons who are shown to be in uneconomic lines of activity. It leaves the majority alone, to advance their productivity according to the same automatic indicators of efficiency, profitability and progress, and with the greatest reliability and calculability of planning for the future. It does not, like inflation, swathe the entire economy in muffling monetary bands which inextricably tie the economic up with the uneconomic, the unproductive with the productive, the efficient with the inefficient. On the contrary, the system of sound money and free competitive enterprise not only indicates; it also separates and segregates the uneconomic and wasteful from the economic and productive in every line of activity.

The 'social costs' of such a system are therefore well worth bearing. They ensure the most productive functioning, the most rapid technical advance, of the majority of the society's economic activities. Such a swiftly advancing society can better afford to bear the 'social costs' of the swiftest possible adoption of, and adaptation to, new techniques. And its laggard minority will accordingly not lag as long, nor prove as big, as it will under a general, regular, blanketing inflation.

Only Two Ways Ahead

The biggest paradox of inflation is that it brings about the very things which a dynamic society is expected to 'grow out of'. When governments give in to pressure-groups right and left, thus raising costs and prices, they bring about before very long a domestic or international crisis of their currency. From such crises there are only two ways of escape.

The first is the inflationary way. It involves more monetary 'shots in the arm' to cover the rising costs. Before very long this involves devaluation of the currency, which upsets domestic and foreign contracts and all calculations for the future. Democratic governments therefore try hard not to let inflation bring too frequent crises and devaluations, since if it does the whole society becomes the opposite of dynamic and growing. It lags, limps and staggers along.

Accordingly this paradox emerges: even when democratic governments timidly or deliberately choose inflation, they try most of the time to keep it under control. Now the means of control over the rate of inflation is in essence the second way of escape from it; only in this case the escape is never complete. As long as a government goes on inflating, it will find it will have to use the means at its command to prevent the stream of purchasing power from too rapidly outrunning the stream of things available to purchasers. Those means are mainly of two kinds: monetary and fiscal.

The first consists of all measures controlling the flow of money from its various *sources*: the government's own short-term borrowings, the banks' advances to their customers, the volume of hire-purchase contracts, State undertakings' attitudes to wage demands from their workpeople, the simultaneous or consequent attitudes of employers in private enterprise to theirs, etc. So this first means of governmental control over a continuing inflation entails what is called 'a national (*i.e.* governmental) wage policy', as well as the more familiar controls over the flow of money and credit. And that entails a much greater governmental control over all wages and over all trade unions and their activities than most democracies have hitherto been prepared to consider. (Australia, with her long history of inflation, has had to institute it, though it frequently causes paralytic convulsions of her economy.) It is significant that today more and more voices are raised in America, Germany, Britain, France, Scandinavia, Holland, etc, declaring or demanding that their governments should institute 'a national wage policy' together with extensive new controls over trade unions. This is the logical outcome of continuous inflation. It is dictated by a very natural, widespread, political demand by all other groups in the democracy for social justice, provoked by the obvious preferential treatment secured by trade unions for their members through industrial (and political) organization. Social and political stresses stemming from inflationary injustice thus become increasingly dangerous the longer the inflation continues. And the longer it continues, the more severely will governments eventually be constrained to control the pressure-groups securing preferential (*i.e.* unjust) treatment.

The second kind of governmental control is not over the various sources of the monetary flow, but over its *spending* once it has become people's incomes. It is therefore in essence taxing people's purchasing power back from them. It is accordingly a fiscal control. It can be imposed on inflationary profits; on weekly pay-packets in workplaces as well as all other incomes; on goods and services as purchase tax, entertainments tax, turn-over taxes, etc; and even on capital as a capital levy. Its object is to whisk back from people and businesses part or all of their inflationary gains of purchasing power, in order to safeguard the currency. Thus this second, fiscal kind of control over the rate of inflation really makes nonsense of the whole inflationary exercise. It is only frequent because people do not understand how inflation works; but governments understand it only too well. They get hold of the whisked-back purchasing-power for their own inflationary ends. Those ends include paying deficits or other subsidies to various State undertakings and their employees. Accordingly this second, fiscal means of control over inflation also creates social injustices and political stresses. And it does not make for steady, dynamic growth in a democracy because political pressure is always on the government to disburse its fiscal gains—its whisk-back—as grants, subsidies, deficits, welfare services, and all other forms of consumption by someone or other. In short, the fiscal control further burdens the taxpayers but fails to effect a cure.

Clearly, the least nonsensical, most dynamic, most democratically just procedure is to avoid inflation from the outset, or to halt it in its tracks if it is already under way. It is to preserve sound, calculable, and for the medium-to-long term reliable, purchasing power. It is to keep money as 'neutral' as possible, so that all other factors in society—economic or not—can be assessed and valued without any need to wonder whether the monetary measuring-rod itself is varying, in which way, to what extent, and at what rate. To achieve that, the safest and best way is for the government of a democracy to control the flow of purchasing power at its sources: the first means of control described above.

The second, fiscal means of control over spending should then seldom, if ever, become necessary.

Competitive Efficiency

Inflation means arbitrary favouritism, preferential treatment, and creation of vested interests. It veils natural costs and therefore confuses calculations. Consequently the cure for it involves increasing competition, reducing protection, and exposing vested interests and veiled costs to natural economic breezes. Those breezes will arise inside a country as soon as it starts to remove shields from vested interests. But they will also blow into it from outside. Hence one cure for inflation—recently demonstrated in Australia, but not yet by the United States or Britain—is to reduce tariffs and let more competitive foreign products into the inflation-ridden country. Then natural values re-emerge and reliable calculations can be made.

But this cure for inflation by greater competition must be comprehensive. It is idle to let more foreign goods in, while keeping up inflation and domestic subsidies and other protective devices at home for the vested interests of farmers, trade unions, fuel producers and manufacturers. That way extra competition will only mean more and louder squeals for more and faster protection. More and faster inflation will then probably result. The cure for inflation must therefore comprise from the outset a domestic policy of reducing the degree of protectionism, subsidizing, and tenderness towards vested interests at home.

Such a diminution of protection for vested interests spells some immediate unemployment of economic resources: of men, materials and machines. That sudden, transitional unemployment exactly measures the amount of *uneconomic* activity which went on in the phase of over-full employment. But it need only be sudden and transitional. Once it is completed, and once monetary inflation is stopped, the country's system gets down to the natural economic values, costs and prices. All calculations from then onwards are more reliable, less confused.

Clearly the cure of inflation can more easily be effected in a purely domestic setting. International agreement to halt inflation by simultaneous action is hard even to imagine, though necessary and desirable. Accordingly, countries only involved in foreign trade to a small extent (*e.g.* the United States and France) stand better chances of overcoming inflation than those (*e.g.* Britain, Holland, Germany, Switzerland, Sweden) in whose national incomes foreign trade bulks large. The reason, of course, is that a government's writ to stop inflation can easily be made to run within its own jurisdiction, but it cannot be made to run in those of foreigners; and they probably will not agree to do the same counter-inflationary things at the same time.

If country A is countering inflation and letting in more of country B's goods, while country B isn't countering inflation, country A's currency at first will be more on offer (to pay for B's goods). A's balance of payments at first will go askew, as it owes more. But if inflation persists in B (and C and D and so on) and is really countered in A, prices in B, C, D, etc will go on rising, while they won't in A. Then people in B, C, D, etc will increasingly buy in A, while the people in A buy less and less abroad (since A prices remain lower). So A's balance of payments difficulties will very quickly be overcome as its currency is more demanded by B, C, D, etc. So A's currency will soon appreciate against those of B, C, D, etc. Thus a country substantially involved in international trade needs a substantial reserve of gold and international currencies to tide it over the initial period when it is stopping inflation. But once the tide-over period is ended, it will tend to buy less, and sell more, abroad (as its currency appreciates).

This is precisely the experience of Germany between 1950 and 1958. Only in 1958 did the pressure increase upon Germany to reduce her unnecessary industrial and agricultural protection (tariffs and quotas), by which time the preferential treatment for the goods of her other five partners in 'the Six' of the European Common Market was beginning. And only in 1959 did it become apparent that in fact Germany had levied a toll on the rest of the world—principally on the United States and Britain—by *not inflating as much as the rest*. What led to the re-emergence of an inflationary threat in Germany in 1959-60 was not her internal process of countering inflation but her continuation, for far too long and at too high rates, of protectionism for her farmers and industrialists. Germany secured great profit from countering inflation; but it largely went to feed an artificial boom behind protective barriers against other countries' goods; and so inflation re-entered by the back door.

The moral is obvious. Freer trade and more competitive enterprise must go with the purely monetary actions to counter inflation. That is why all apologists for inflation demand, with it, State controls, restrictions, and regulations of all trade and enterprise.

Stopping Inflation

There are only two ways to stop continuous inflation. Both are needed at once:

(1) to cut down the pressure of new money and credit, by cutting Government and State expenditure to fit reasonable tax revenues (such as give people of *all* classes and incomes incentives) and to fit the available savings which the State and private enterprise can borrow at free market rates of interest, at medium or long term; and

(2) to raise productive efficiency (productivity) in all walks of economic life, by cutting down restrictive practices of all kinds, by improving managerial techniques and training, and by getting more modern machines *and then letting them turn out all they are capable of producing* (which means revising both trade unionists' and managements' attitudes to shift-work, organization, machinery, managerial methods, etc).

If a country pushed ahead with these two methods of combating inflation at once, its costs would remain stable or fall, not rise. The first is the government's responsibility and within its power. The second is that of trade unions and management and within their power. Once costs and prices were stabilized, the currency would be safer. Savings would increase. So would investment. The overdue improvements its people wanted would begin to come about—modern railways, highways, technical schools, hospitals, etc, and the development of overseas resources in the less industrialized nations. The balance of payments would be assured by more rapidly rising productive efficiency. Reserves would mount. And last but not least—indeed, from our own personal and national viewpoints the prime benefit of all— social, political and industrial tensions would relax. Our natural, justified differences of aim or policy could be argued out and carried out, without wrecking the whole ship in the breakers ahead. The rot in its timbers would have been stopped.

That is not an impossible task for a democracy. It need not demand longer or harder work—only better work, better organized, better managed, in up-to-date ways. It need not imply falling sales, falling wages, rising unemployment. On the contrary; it is the quickest foreseeable way to get rising sales, rising real incomes all round, and full employment, together with reliable money, stable prices, worthwhile savings, and modernization (investment).

It is a task jointly to be undertaken by State industries, the government, and private enterprise. That means it must jointly and simultaneously be supported by politicians of all parties and the people who elect them, and by trade unionists and managements on the crucial industrial front. It must be understood by the men in the street, so that no one need ever see men on the street again. It must be willed and wanted—this determination and policy to beat inflation—like the winning of a war, *by all people*. For if they do not band together to beat it, it will beat them.

The primary duty is the government's, for they control the spending and programmes of the State, and the supply (and quality) of the money and credit and therefore of the currency.

Let them limit the creation of money and credit. Let them ensure the stability of money by giving non-political monetary authorities independent powers to criticize and to safeguard the currency. Let them stop financing their own programmes by floating debt. Better than having physical controls and ubiquitous rationing leading to widespread inefficiency, let the State cut its coat from available savings. Let the government reduce taxes, but induce individuals and institutions to save more; and then let them borrow all they need at medium or long term in free and open capital markets.

Any shortages of money, savings, etc, would then only be felt 'at the margin'—in a firm or a place here or there, in a section or part of an industry—and not in an entire nation clamped under irons. An enduring, general increase in unemployment need not then occur. Whenever unemployment of the nation's resources then occurred, it would be a true index of inefficiency, waste, out-of-dateness, or unnecessary activity. And it could be looked after by such national measures as have been outlined above.[1]

If the leading democracies don't or won't stop the inflationary rot in their timbers it will sink them, while other nations sail ahead. It will be poor consolation for their political parties, managements and unions to say as the ship sinks 'Anyway, the leak was at the other end of the boat.'

[1] See pp. 143-8.

CHAPTER 10

DANGER AHEAD

The examples we took from the Roman world—and many more we can find in the medieval, Renaissance and modern world—emphasize society's growing dependence on capital formation, saving in all its forms, and on the long-run reliability of a standard of value.

Consider how little was the real capital, the productive equipment, of the ancient and medieval world, up to only 150 years ago. The horse was the only local means of locomotion until this century, at least by land. Yet in the last sixty years we in the West —who account even now for only one-sixth of mankind, and only one quarter if we include Soviet Russia and its European satellites—possess virtually all the capital of the world. There is little productive capital south of the equator. Yet we, like the underdeveloped world, demand more capital. We invent more opportunities for its use; and in so doing—and inflating meanwhile—we make the worldwide shortage of capital worse.

Never in human history have three trends coincided as they now do:

(1) the lengthening of the expectation of individual lives at birth by applications of medical science all over the globe, simultaneously;

(2) the simultaneous demands all over the globe, due to technical progress in communications, et cetera, for rapid increases in productive capital per man; and

(3) the simultaneous demands all over the globe, due to these and other reasons, for equally rapid increases in consumption per man.

Hitherto in history—even in the history of the relatively slow inflation in Western Europe flowing from the import of the New World's precious metals in the sixteenth century—the effects of an inflation, even a fairly rapid one (*e.g.* Germany, Hungary, France between the wars) have been confined to a nation or a society more or less immediately affected. But that has manifestly not been true since the last war.

Some national inflations have been faster than others; for instance, that of France has been faster than that of Britain; that of Britain faster than those of Germany, Switzerland, the United States, Canada, Venezuela. But throughout the trading world on our Western side of the Iron Curtain, the inflation flowing from the simultaneity of the three above-mentioned factors has been steady and progressive. Nor is there much sign that it will be politically brought under control as a matter of international governmental and administrative responsibility. Nor, indeed, is there much sign that democratic and representative governments (at any rate) will control it *in the long run*, however much or little they contrive to check it in the short run. Totalitarian States seem better at controlling it, but at the cost to their consumers and producers of controlling everything else and everyone in the State.

Accordingly we must be prepared for some explosive economic situation both within and between our Western nations whenever worldwide inflation gets loose again. Such an explosive economic situation in the contemporary world must also mean some pretty explosive political situations. Consider the mixture.

First there are the three factors I have mentioned as being at work all over the globe today—rapidly growing populations and lengthening lives, rapidly growing demands for productive (or investment) capital, and equally rapidly growing demands for consumer goods everywhere.

Secondly, at the rates we have clocked-up in the leading industrial nations of the West in the past fifteen years alone, such an inflation puts a premium on consumption and militates against the very saving which is the cure of the inflation.

Thirdly, being worldwide among us in the West, this inflation seems almost unsusceptible of *national* control, while our political and administrative institutions—particularly in economic affairs —are not yet sufficiently developed for an *international* agreement to end inflation, by due stabilizations and controls of monetary supplies, to be reached.

Fourthly, our technological progress has become so rapid and internationally all-embracing that scarcely one nation among us —and certainly not a leading industrial nation—can contract-out of such inflationary circumstances.

And fifth and lastly, in the light of these ingredients in the mixture, it remains difficult to damp down inflation politically. In democracies it seems easier to copy the 'antique Roman' manner—to buy the votes of those groups and classes who are doing well out of high taxes and inflation, to let the long-run reliability of the standard of value diminish, and to plaster-over any cracks in the social fabric (*e.g.* injustice to pensioners, holders of Government bonds, etc) by belated and random palliatives.

Inflation as Social Policy

If we look around us we can recognize many symptoms of the social disease of inflation such as one finds *mutatis mutandis* in every society which has suffered it. But we now see them on a cosmic scale. There is no need to emphasize the injustices—even more, the wastes and inefficiencies—of such inflations as we have had in Europe since the war: the advantaging of debtors, the pillaging *per contra* of creditors, the bureaucratic centralizations necessitated by governments unable to arrest (but willing to mask the symptoms of) inflation, the significant emergence of 'gold clauses' and what the French call *indexisation* for State and other loans at fixed interest, the absurdity of demanding more internal and international lending at fixed interest in the light of what has been happening to recent lenders, and the pervasive distrust of *all* money in economic transactions.

The equivalents of Roman legionaries in modern democracies are the politically or industrially organized mass of 'the workers'. Their votes put democratic Governments in or out. Political parties strive to buy those votes with the proceeds of repetitive raids on the property or earnings of the more responsible, more skilled, more productive minority. So a new privileged but unresponsible class is born, at the cost of the providers of that productive capital and know-how whereon economic progress depends. As private capital is eroded by inflation or raided by the State, a delightful mass-consumption seems like an enduring dynamic prosperity. But it is not dynamic; it is not reliable; and it is abruptly punctuated by recurrent monetary and other economic crises, both national and international; for the nations do not co-ordinate even their inflations. In dictatorships, paradoxically enough, the long-run reliability of their standards of value is more carefully (if forcibly) safeguarded, while their productive minority is relatively better rewarded. Thus we and our one-time opponents approximate, but travelling in opposite directions.

Stable Prices and Stable Societies

In the light of the trends already mentioned, what are our real needs—inside our still largely free societies in the West, and between all of them?

First, a standard of value reliable enough in the fairly long run to permit calculations of risks and to encourage saving and investment.

Secondly, an agreed international system—facilitated by governments positively, and negatively by their allowing a natural system to work—under which both borrowers and lenders can calculate risks and rewards in reliable monetary terms, *i.e.* in reliable *real* terms.

And thirdly, a far wider recognition that the Russians face precisely the same economic problems as we do in the West: namely, getting the savings, raising the productive efficiency, investing in underdeveloped territories, raising people's consumption, writing-off and replacing old with more and better capital, rewarding 'top talents' adequately, and so on.

Surely it is time we proclaimed the economic lesson of inflations in history, and of Russia's economic development these past forty years. That lesson is this: you can inflate and expropriate former *élites* and privileged groups out of their property and their existence; you can benefit new privileged classes; but you cannot rapidly develop even a totalitarian State (like Russia) or a totalitarian empire of client-States (like that of the Russians) without managerial *élites*, encouragements to enterprisers, and some going-without of consumption on the part of the mass of consumers. Surely we ought to teach this lesson to our own electorates. Surely the social and administrative—even the political—upheavals in Russia in the last few years, after all the

Russian people and their rulers have been through, show that economic calculability, monetary dependability, and the reliability of standards of value are the prerequisites of a dynamic society and of economic progress.

There seems to be precious little choice open to us between being democratically reasonable—that is, securing sound money and a free economy—and, on the other hand, attempting to get much the same economic results by totalitarian controls, force, blood and iron. If you try to straddle the two, you only get an inefficient, static, collectivist catastrophe: which is how a Socialism pledged to inflation appears as contrasted with Communism. It seems that too many of our Western intellectuals are crossing to the Russian side of the street just when Russian intellectuals, having trodden it long and painfully enough, have started to cross to ours. One can comprehend, though not support, the economics and politics of a 100 per cent totalitarianism. One can neither comprehend nor support those of an inflationary Socialism which spells social collapse into an eventual and inescapable totalitarianism.

Conclusion of the Matter

The working-out of inflations in history caused big social changes and injustices, from which (however) little, if any, real economic progress, little social dynamics, came. In some cases, especially that of Rome, the entire social fabric and civilization came down in ruins, and on the ruins little was built for over a millennium. In a few cases—that of sixteenth-century Spain— the continuation of steady inflation was not so much due to political cowardice or ineptitude as to sheer ignorance of the causes. But in most cases of uninterrupted, progressive and rapid inflation—from ancient Rome to modern Germany—the causes were appreciated, the inflation became policy, and the government utilized it for purposes of politics, *i.e.* of power. The ends of such policy-inflations were socially cataclysmic. Their outcomes were unplanned, though predictable.

That prospect still faces us in the now-interdependent trading world of the West. What happened in the American and West German economies in 1959-60 is but an indication. The built-in causes of inflation still operate: 'full employment' and inflation still seem synonymous. Yet we still face a choice, not a deterministic fate. The choice seems to be between an unplanned, really unwanted, but nevertheless inescapable social cataclysm, caused by deliberate prolongation of progressive inflation beyond the point of toleration by all classes of taxpayers, on the one hand; and on the other, reasoned and reasonable agreements—within and between our leading countries—to restore long-run reliability to standards of value.

True, if we make the latter choice, our peoples and their governments, groupings, vested interests, etc, will have to bear the practical implications of such rationality and reliability in both domestic and international affairs. These practical implications are what makes democracy difficult to run, politically, in one country; and what makes co-operation between democracies so difficult. What do the masses of our citizens, and their competing political leaders, really want? This challenge must be repeatedly and publicly put before them.

If, in fear of taking the difficult choice, they take the easier inflationary one, they will soon bring about the social and international upheavals already described—both in history, and as possibilities in the not-too-long-run future—as cataclysmic, abrupt, and uncontrollable. Planned, progressive inflation as a policy ends in unplanned, unwanted, but inescapable—and, above all, unforeseen—disaster. That is the lesson of all inflations in history.